NEW DIRECTIONS FOR PROGRAM EVALUATION
A Publication of the American Evaluation Association

William R. Shadish, *Memphis State University*
EDITOR-IN-CHIEF

Hard-Won Lessons in Program Evaluation

Michael Scriven
Western Michigan University

AUTHOR

Number 58, Summer 1993

JOSSEY-BASS PUBLISHERS
San Francisco

HARD-WON LESSONS IN PROGRAM EVALUATION
Michael Scriven (author)
New Directions for Program Evaluation, no. 58
William R. Shadish, Editor-in-Chief

Microfilm copies of issues and articles are available in 16mm and 35mm,
as well as microfiche in 105mm, through University Microfilms Inc., 300
North Zeeb Road, Ann Arbor, Michigan 48106.

LC 85-644749   ISSN 0164-7989   ISBN 1-55542-697-2

NEW DIRECTIONS FOR PROGRAM EVALUATION is part of The Jossey-Bass
Education Series and is published quarterly by Jossey-Bass Inc., Publishers
(publication number USPS 449-050).

EDITORIAL CORRESPONDENCE should be sent to the editor-in-chief, William R.
Shadish, Department of Psychology, Memphis State University, Memphis,
Tennessee 38152.

The paper used in this journal is acid-free and meets the strictest
guidelines in the United States for recycled paper (50 percent
recycled waste, including 10 percent post-consumer waste).
Manufactured in the United States of America.

INSTRUCTIONS TO CONTRIBUTORS

NEW DIRECTIONS FOR PROGRAM EVALUATION (NDPE), a quarterly sourcebook, is an official publication of the American Evaluation Association. As such, NDPE publishes empirical, methodological, and theoretical work on all aspects of program evaluation and related fields. Substantive areas may include any area of social programming such as mental health, education, job training, medicine, or public health, but may also extend the boundaries of evaluation to such topics as product evaluation, personnel evaluation, policy analysis, or technology assessment. In all cases, the focus on evaluation is more important than the particular substantive topic.

NDPE does not consider or publish unsolicited single manuscripts. Each issue of NDPE is devoted to a single topic, with contributions solicited, organized, reviewed, and edited by a guest editor. Issues may take any of several forms, such as a series of related chapters, a monograph, or a long article followed by brief critical commentaries. In all cases, proposals must follow a specific format, which can be obtained from the editor-in-chief. These proposals are sent to members of the editorial board, and to relevant substantive experts, for peer review. This process may result in rejection, acceptance, or a recommendation to revise and resubmit. However, NDPE is committed to working constructively with potential guest editors to help them develop acceptable proposals. Close contact with the editor-in-chief is encouraged during proposal preparation and generation.

COPIES OF NDPE's "Guide for Proposal Development" and "Proposal Format" can be obtained from the editor-in-chief:

William R. Shadish, Editor-in-Chief
New Directions for Program Evaluation
Department of Psychology
Memphis State University
Memphis, TN 38152
Office: 901-678-4687
FAX: 901-678-2579
Bitnet: SHADISHWR@MEMSTVX1

CONTENTS

Author's Notes

Perhaps the best way to convey a feeling for the real stuff in evaluation is to examine the mistakes that we have made and what we have learned from them. The end result of this approach is a list of points negating something that seemed at first to make sense. This kind of list looks a little different from the usual list of key points in an area, which tries to be more positive and systematic, but most of the items end up being boring. The reason they are boring is that in evaluation, as in many other areas—for example, philosophy, psychology, and economics—general theses about the subject matter are to a considerable degree extensions of common sense. After all, everyone in his or her own practical life does some evaluation and some psychology, philosophy, and economics, and they have listened to a good deal of advice from their parents and teachers—and the media—about how to do these tasks properly. The catch is that all of this commonsense advice supports conflicting adages (for example, "The evaluator should be unbiased" and "It is impossible to avoid all biases"), and when we get down to a specific case, it quite often turns out that following one or more of the alternatives is an expensive mistake. The way in which most of the "lessons" are phrased in this volume, *Hard-Won Lessons in Program Evaluation,* so that commonsense adages are contradicted, may therefore be more interesting than the usual approach because there is still something seductive about the old errors.

Only the first of the thirty-one "theses" presented is dealt with in any detail due to space limitations. However, the introduction and the treatment of the first thesis present a new general view of evaluation that provides a basis for many of the other theses. (Indeed, the brevity of the treatment of the later points provides a long-awaited excuse to use a version of that paralyzing comment from the G. H. Hardy era of texts in pure mathematics: "Demonstration of this result is left to the reader as an exercise." Despite the limitations, my aim here is to provide a substantial introduction to what is intended to be the most analytical and comprehensive of the various approaches to modern program evaluation and management.[1]

This volume developed from a talk given at the National Science Foundation (NSF) early in 1992 for staff from eight agencies concerned with the evaluation of education programs in the fields of science, mathematics, engineering, and technology. Many thanks to Ken Travers, head of the NSF Office of Research, Evaluation, and Development in the Education Directorate, for the invitation to give the talk and the AERA Senior Fellowship that supported this work, and to his staff for their cooperation in improving it. This material has also benefited considerably from comments by Morris Lai, Will Shadish, Bob Stake, and John Mergendoller on earlier versions.

To assist the reader, I provide the following outline of the thirty-one theses:

Chapter 1. The Nature of Evaluation
  1. Program evaluation is not a determination of goal attainment.
  2. Program evaluation is not applied social science.
  3. Program evaluation is neither a dominant nor an autonomous field of evaluation.

Chapter 2. Implications for Popular Evaluation Approaches
  4. Side effects are often the main point.
  5. Subject matter expertise may be the right hand of education program and proposal evaluation, but one cannot wrap things up with a single hand.
  6. Evaluation designs without provision for evaluation of the evaluation are unclear on the concept.
  7. An evaluation without a recommendation is like a fish without a bicycle.

Chapter 3. Implications for Popular Models of Program Evaluation
  8. Pure outcome evaluation usually yields too little too late, and pure process evaluation is usually invalid or premature.
  9. Noncomparative evaluations are comparatively useless.
  10. Formative evaluation is attractive, but summative evaluation is imperative.
  11. Rich description is not an approach to program evaluation but a retreat from it.
  12. One can only attain fourth-generation evaluation by counting backward.

Chapter 4. Intermediate Evaluation Design Issues
  13. Merit and quality are not the same as worth or value.
  14. Different evaluation designs are usually required for ranking, grading, scoring, and apportioning.
  15. Needs assessments provide some but not all of the values needed for evaluations.
  16. Money costs are hard to determine—but they are the easy part of cost analysis.
  17. Program evaluation should begin with the presuppositions of the program and sometimes go no further.
  18. Establishing statistical significance is the easy part of establishing significance.
  19. "Pulling it all together" is where most evaluations fall apart.

Chapter 5. An Advanced Evaluation Design Issue: Beyond Validity
  20. Validity does not ensure credibility.
  21. Validity and credibility do not ensure utility.

22. Even utilization does not ensure utility.
23. Program evaluation involves research and ends with a report, but research reports are negative paradigms for evaluation reports.

Chapter 6. An Advanced Evaluation Management Issue: Bias Control
24. Preference and commitment do not entail bias.
25. The usual agency counsel's criteria for avoidance of conflict of interest select for ignorance, low contributions, indecisiveness, or some combination thereof.
26. Program officers are biased toward favorable findings.
27. External evaluators are biased toward favorable findings.
28. Peer review panels are unreliable, fashion-biased, and manipulable.

Chapter 7. Parting Perspectives
29. The most difficult problems with program evaluation are not methodological or political but psychological.
30. Evaluation is as important as content in education programs.
31. Routine program evaluation should pay for itself.

Some caveats are warranted. First, the term *program evaluation* has become a label for a limited approach, covering only part of what is required in order to do adequate program evaluation, just as *needs assessment* has, in some quarters, become a name for a formalized approach that covers only part of what is required in order to determine needs. In this volume, there are also comments and theses about proposal evaluation, evaluation management, personnel and product evaluation, the evaluation of evaluations, and the general nature of evaluation—because all of these are essential parts of serious program evaluation. A widening of one's perspective on program evaluation helps one to avoid reinvention of the wheel and omission of relevant aspects of what one is supposed to be evaluating.

Second, the lessons here are specific to or particularly important to evaluation. They do not cover the basic design of experiments, some understanding of which is presupposed.

Third, these theses were not deduced from a preexisting general theory—as was statistics from probability theory—but rather were inferred from analysis of practice, in spite of strong opposition to the very possibility of any such discipline as evaluation. We now have the beginnings of a general theory, but it has been developed only about as far as where game theory was twenty-five years ago.

Fourth, these theses refer to (what is claimed to be) best practice; the state of common practice is a long way from reaching that level. Most of the mistakes listed here are still incorporated in what currently passes for evaluation in many state and federal agencies, and in private firms and philanthropies. We have learned better at considerable cost in time, money, achievements, and quality—but not everyone has yet learned. The lag time in implementation is substantial for the usual reasons: It takes at least two generations to replace the old guard in any field, since they control the recommendations network and train their own replacements. It seems certain that less than half the people doing evaluations—or designing, managing, or monitoring them—have had formal training in evaluation, or have made a serious study of the literature, or belong to the professional associations, or subscribe to the journals. A guess would place the proportion at around 20 percent. Still fewer of their supervisors have had that training, since they are yet further removed from the graduate programs that have incorporated elements of evaluation training; hence they lack appropriate standards by which to commission or judge evaluation work done by others, or to identify needed training in their subordinates.

Fifth, even among those that have had training in evaluation or have developed and published theories from their own backgrounds, it is unlikely that a majority would agree that the perspective here represents the state of the art. As one might expect, the infancy of a new discipline is a time when radically different views of its nature are still widespread. For evaluation, the situation has been exacerbated by the taboo on the subject, which, as in the case of sex research or parapsychology, leads to some fairly bizarre theories. Some of these differences are spelled out in what follows, because evaluators have often encountered, or will in the future encounter, representatives of other viewpoints (or evaluation reports from them), and it is helpful to have the contrasts highlighted. So, the thirty-one theses are propositions that I view as hard-won by the field, whereas others may see them as claims to be denied rather than learned. The strength of these theses, such as it is, must reside in the reasons for them, and to understand those reasons we must first look at their precursors.

Michael Scriven
Author

MICHAEL SCRIVEN was the first president of what is now the American Evaluation Association and founding editor of its journal, which is now Evaluation Practice. *His current appointments include consulting professor at Stanford University's Graduate School of Education, adjunct professor of philosophy at Western Michigan University, professor at the Pacific Graduate School of Psychology, and senior AERA fellow at the National Science Foundation.*

Historical positions on the nature of evaluation are briefly characterized. A systematic approach then addresses the questions that clients need answered but which could not be answered by most of these models. The answers add up to a more general account of program evaluation and a more general view of evaluation across all disciplines.

The Nature of Evaluation

Past Conceptions of Evaluation

With the following simplified classification, I identify five views or approaches that are alternatives to the one explored here. They are listed below in the order of their emergence into a position of power in the field of program evaluation since the mid 1960s, when the explosive phase in the field's development began. In addition to those discussed, there is a range of exotica—fascinating and illuminating theories ranging from the jurisprudential to the connoisseurship models—that I pass over here for reasons of space.

Strong Decision Support View. This approach was an explication of the use of program evaluation as part of the process of rational program management. The approach, implicit in management practice for millennia, has two versions. The strong version described here conceived of evaluators as those doing investigations designed to arrive at *evaluative conclusions to assist the decision maker.* Supporters of this approach pay considerable attention to whether programs reach their goals, but they go beyond that concern into questions about whether the goals match the needs that they are supposedly addressing, thereby differentiating themselves from the much narrower relativistic approach discussed later in this volume. The strong decision support view is exemplified in the work of Ralph Tyler (although he is often wrongly thought of as having never questioned program goals) and extensively elaborated in the Context, Input, Process, and Product (CIPP) model of evaluation. The CIPP model goes beyond the rhetoric of decision support into checklists covering most of what is involved in program evaluation and uses them to infer evaluative conclusions (see Stufflebeam, 1971). Daniel Stufflebeam, who helped to formulate the CIPP model, has continued to play a leading role in evaluation, still representing—and further developing—this perspective. By contrast, Egon Guba, one of his cocollaborators in the early CIPP work, has now gone in a quite different direction (see the constructivist approach below).

Weak Decision Support View. The preceding approach has often been described as *the* decision support approach, but there is another approach that also claims that title. It holds that decision support stops short of drawing evaluative conclusions or critiquing program goals. This point of view is represented by evaluation theorists such as Marvin Alkin, who define evaluation as factual data gathering in the service of a decision maker who is to draw the evaluative conclusions.[2] This position is popular among those who think that true science cannot or should not make value judgments.

Relativistic View. This is another position that is somewhat more like evaluation as we normally think of it, although it still manages to avoid drawing evaluative conclusions. This is the view that evaluation should be done by using the client's values as a framework, without any judgment by the evaluator about those values or any reference to other values. This view is discussed under Theses 1, 2, and 3 below. The most widely used text in evaluation is by Rossi and Freeman (1989), two social scientists, and essentially represents this approach. The weak decision support view and the relativistic view were the vehicles that allowed social scientists to join the program evaluation bandwagon. (By contrast, the strong decision support view was put forward by education researchers, who were less committed to the paradigm of values-free social science, possibly because their discipline includes the history and philosophy of education, comparative education, and education administration, which have quite different paradigms.) The simplest form of this approach was developed into the discrepancy model of program evaluation by Malcolm Provus (the discrepancies being divergences from the projected task and time line for the project). Program monitoring, as it is often done, comes very close to the discrepancy model. My reasons for thinking that this approach is a long way from evaluation are given below under Thesis 1; only a few of them involve validation of program goals.

Rich Description Approach. According to this view, evaluation could be done as a kind of ethnographic or journalistic enterprise in which the evaluators report what they see without trying to make evaluative statements or infer to evaluative conclusions, not even in terms of the client's values (as the relativist does). This view has been very widely supported by Robert Stake, the North Dakota school, many of the U.K. theorists, and others. It is briefly discussed under Thesis 11 below. It usually has a flavor of relativism and sometimes looks like a precursor of the constructivist approach described below.

Social Process School. This approach crystallized about twelve years ago, approximately halfway to the present moment in the history of the emerging discipline, through the work of a distinguished group of Stanford academics led by Lee Cronbach (see Cronbach and others, 1980). It is notable for its rejection of the importance of evaluation in providing support for decisions about programs and in ensuring accountability (that is, summative evaluation), and the substitution of understanding social programs for evaluating them in the ordinary sense.[3] Their position, like mine, is encapsulated in a set of theses, and comments about their theses recur throughout this volume. This volume may in fact represent an implementation of the eighty-seventh thesis in their list: "There is need for exchanges [about evaluation] more energetic than the typical academic discussion and more responsible than debate among partisans" (Cronbach and others, 1980)—if indeed there is any such middle ground. Ernest House, a highly independent thinker about evaluation, also stressed the importance of the social ambience but was quite distinctive in his stress on the ethical and argumentation dimensions of evaluation. In fact, his stress on the ethical dimension was intended as a counterpoint to the absence of this concern in Cronbach and others (1980) (see House, 1980).

Constructivist, or Fourth-Generation, Approach. This approach represents the most recent riders on the front of the wave, notably Egon Guba and Yvonna Lincoln, but with many other supporters, including a strong following among U.S. and U.K. evaluators. This point of view rejects evaluation as the search for quality, merit, worth, and so on, in favor of the idea that it—and all "truth"—is the result of construction by individuals and negotiation by groups (see Thesis 12 below).

Commentary. Now, the commonsense view of program evaluation is probably that it is the sort of thing that doctors, road testers, engineers, and interviewers do, but with the subject matter of programs instead of patients, cars, structures, or applicants, respectively. The results of this kind of investigation are, of course, direct evaluative conclusions, such as "The patient [program] has improved slightly under the new therapeutic [managerial] regime." Of the views listed above, the strong decision support view, of which CIPP is the best-known elaboration, comes closest to a commonsense view of program evaluation.

The CIPP model was a little overgeneralized in that it claimed all (program) evaluation was oriented to decision support. It seems implausible to insist that a historian's evaluation of the "bread and circuses" programs of Roman emperors, or even of the Works Progress Administration, is or should be designed to serve some contemporary decision maker rather than the professional interest of historians and others concerned with the truth about the past. This is the research role of evaluation, the search for truth about merit and worth, its only payoffs being insights. Much of the decision support kind of evaluation, and all of the research type, exemplify what is sometimes called summative evaluation—evaluation of a whole program for the benefit of someone outside the program. One might also argue, contra CIPP, that formative evaluation—evaluation aimed at improving a program or performance, reported back to the program staff—deserves recognition as having a significantly different goal from decision support, and that its importance slightly weakens the claim that evaluation is for decision support. (Of course, it supports decisions about how to improve the program, but that is not the kind of decision that decision support is normally supposed to support.)

The other entries in the list above, that is, almost all schools of thought in evaluation, can be seen as a series of attempts to avoid direct statements about the merit or worth of things. The weak decision support view avoids all evaluative conclusions. The relativistic view avoids direct evaluative claims in favor of relativistic ones.[4] The rich description view avoids direct evaluative claims in favor of nonevaluative descriptions. The social process view avoids them in favor of insights about or understanding of social phenomena. The constructivist view rejects their legitimacy along with that of all other claims. (The connoisseurship model also weakens the evaluative component in evaluation, reducing it to the largely subjective model of a connoisseur's judgments.)

This resistance to the commonsense view of program evaluation, even among those working in the field, has its philosophical roots in the values-free conception of the social sciences, which is discussed shortly, but it also gathered support from another argument, which appears at first sight to be well based on common sense. This was the argument that the decision about whether or not a program is desirable should be made by policymakers, not by evaluators. On this view, it would be presumptuous for program evaluators to act as if it was their job to decide whether the program that they were called in to evaluate should exist.

What is different about the transdisciplinary view advanced in this volume? It extends the commonsense view and is significantly different from the strong decision support view and totally different from all of the other views.

Transdisciplinary View

The name for this view is based on a distinction between primary disciplines—the conventional academic disciplines, crafts, and physical disciplines—and a set of disciplines whose subject matter is some set of or aspect of the tools, methods, and approaches used by the primary disciplines. The transdisciplines include statistics, measurement, logic, and—it is now suggested—evaluation. Each of them is connected to a number of applied fields. Thus, statistics is connected to the applied fields of, for example, biostatistics, statistical mechanics, and demographics. The task of the transdisciplinary approach is not the study of the phenomena in those fields but rather the study of quantitative tools for describing those data. Its results apply across all of the disciplines using, or that should be using, statistics, hence the term *transdiscipline*. Logic, with its applied fields of the logic of the social sciences and so on, is an extremely general transdiscipline, but evaluation is probably the most general (unlike logic, it precedes language); both are much more general than measurement or statistics.

This view, when applied to evaluation, leads to three characteristics that distinguish it from the views on the above list: one epistemological, one political, and one disciplinary. First, it is an *objectivist* view of evaluation. It argues for the idea that evaluation is about the process of determining the merit and worth and so on of, for example, programs, personnel, or products; that these are real, although logically complex, properties of everyday things embedded in a complex relevant context; and that an acceptable degree of objectivity and comprehensiveness in the quest to determine these properties is not only possible but frequently attained. This view contrasts for obvious reasons with all of the other views described earlier, with the exception of the strong decision support view; the contrast with the strong decision support view is in the shift of the primary role from decision serving to truth seeking, with the other roles of evaluation seen as important but not definitional. Since an objectivist position implies that it is part of the evaluator's job to draw direct evaluative conclusions about programs, the position is supported by a head-on attack on the two grounds for avoiding such conclusions. So the position (1) explicitly states and defends the logic of inferring evaluative conclusions from factual and definitional premises and (2) spells out the fallacies in the arguments for the values-free doctrine.

Second, the approach here is a consumer-oriented view rather than a management-oriented approach to program evaluation. This does not mean that it is a consumer advocacy approach in the sense that it only fights for one side in an ancient struggle. It simply regards the consumer's welfare as the primary justification for having a program and accords that welfare the same primacy in the evaluation. That is to say, it rejects decision support—which is support of management decisions—as the main function of evaluation (somewhat in contrast to the strong decision support view), although it aims to provide management decision support as a by-product. Instead, the main function of evaluation is the determination of the merit and worth of programs in terms of how effectively and efficiently they are serving those affected, particularly those receiving, or who should be receiving, the services provided and those who pay for the programs—typically, taxpayers or their representatives. It is appropriate for the welfare of program staff to also receive some weighting, but, for example, schools do not exist primarily as employment centers, so staff welfare (within the constraints of justice) cannot be viewed as of comparable importance to the educational welfare of the students.

To the extent that managers construe service to the consumer as their primary goal, as they normally should if they are managing programs in the public or philanthropic sector, information about the merit or worth of programs is valuable for management decision making (the interest of the two decision support views); and to the extent that the goals of a program reflect the actual needs of consumers, this information approximates feedback about how well the program is meeting its goals (the relativist's concern). But neither of these conditions is treated as a presupposition of an evaluation; they must be investigated and are often violated.

The consumer orientation of the transdisciplinary approach moves us one step beyond establishing the legitimacy of drawing evaluative conclusions in that it argues for the necessity of doing so in many cases. That is, it categorizes any approach as incomplete if it stops short of drawing evaluative conclusions. Practical demonstrations of this principle are in every issue of *Consumer Reports:* The things being evaluated are ranked and graded in a systematic way so that one can see which are the best of the bunch (ranking) and whether the best are safe, good buys, and so on (grading).

Third, the approach here is an overview. It treats program evaluation as merely one of many applied areas within an overarching discipline of evaluation. (These applied areas may also be part of the subject matter of a primary discipline: Personnel evaluation is part of industrial and organizational psychology, biostatistics is part of biology.) This perspective leads to substantial changes in the range of considerations to which program evaluation must pay attention. For example, it must look at other applied evaluation areas for parallels, and to a core discipline for theoretical analyses, but it helps with the added labors by greatly enhancing the methodological repertoire of program evaluation.

Thus, there are two main features of the transdisciplinary approach. The first is the wide-angle emphasis. Here the stress is on (1) the large range of distinctive applied evaluation fields, for example, the leading social science-related entries are program evaluation, product evaluation, personnel evaluation, policy evaluation, performance evaluation, proposal evaluation—the "Big Six"—and meta-evaluation (the evaluation of evaluations); (2) the large range of evaluative processes in fields other than applied evaluation fields, including all of the disciplines (the evaluation of methodologies, information, instruments, research, theories, and so on) and the practical and performing arts (the evaluation of craft skills, compositions, regimens, instructions, and so on); (3) the large range of types of evaluative investigation, from practical levels of evaluation (for example, judging the utility of products or the quality of dives in an Olympic competition) through field program evaluation, to conceptual analysis (for example, the evaluation of the conceptual and theoretical issues in the core discipline of evaluation); and (4) the overlap between the applied fields, which is rarely recognized, for example, methods from one field often solve problems in other fields, yet program evaluation as usually conceived does not include any reference to personnel evaluation, proposal evaluation, or ethical evaluation, each of which must be taken into account in some program evaluations. The second main feature is the technical emphasis. Here the stress is on the idea that evaluation is like statistics and measurement in that it requires special knowledge and skills training. It is different from them in that it is far more multidisciplinary. For example, more than a dozen subdisciplines are involved in just the one applied field of program evaluation, more than half of them not covered in any typical doctoral training program in any other discipline such as sociology, psychology, law, or accounting.

Why should one believe this view? Examination of the credentials of the many authors supporting one or another of the other views does little to resolve the issue, because credentials from other fields (for example, educational testing, logic, philosophy, psychology, and sociology), which the advocates of the other positions have in abundance, are about as relevant as a Nobel Prize in physics is to someone's views about abortion rights. Instead, the credibility of the transdisciplinary view depends on the merit of the reasons that I offer in its support here. Note that once one is convinced that there is some common logic of evaluation, something like the process that we see in product evaluation, then one must conclude that the discipline of evaluation transcends the boundaries of particular applied fields such as program evaluation. This conclusion makes the above-described views, from the weak decision support approach to the constructivist approach, extremely implausible; are individuals really going to cancel their subscriptions to *Consumer Reports* on the grounds that it is just reporting its own opinions or should just be describing without evaluating?

Program evaluation treated in isolation can be seen in the ways that the alternative positions advocate; program evaluation treated as just one more application of the procedures that lead us to solid evaluative results in product evaluation can hardly be seen as consistent with the flight from direct evaluative conclusions that those positions embody. While there are special features of program evaluation that often make it less straightforward than the simpler kind of product evaluation, the reverse is often the case. The view that it is different from *all* product evaluation is only popular among those who know little about product evaluation. For example, the idea that program evaluation is inherently much more political than product evaluation is common but wrong; the history of the interstate highway system and the superconducting supercollider are counterexamples, and it was after all "only" a product evaluation—commissioned by Congress and done flawlessly—that led to the dismissal of the director of the National Bureau of Standards.[5]

Shadow of the Values-Free Doctrine

Here, I warn about a common but serious misconception that, if not pointed out, is likely to lead to a misunderstanding of the significance of everything that follows in this volume. The modern era of program evaluation—a term that here includes project evaluation as a special case—began about twenty-five years ago, and it began as late as it did in intellectual history because of the taboo on evaluation imposed by the values-free doctrine in the social sciences. Although it is fashionable today to think that we have discarded the values-free doctrine, that conclusion is just part of shoddy, "politically correct" thinking in marginal intellectual circles.

This view that we have outgrown the values-free doctrine is dangerous because it is based on a complete misrepresentation of the doctrine, and hence on a pseudorefutation. The doctrine has not in fact been discarded by many, probably most, of the methodologically sophisticated social scientists who are leaders in their fields—certainly not in their private thinking. The reason that it is still powerful is that there are strong prima facie reasons for thinking that it is true, reasons not addressed by the usual refutations.

The straw-man version of the values-free doctrine that has been "refuted" is so far off the mark that it does not seem to have been maintained by anyone in the entire history of the social sciences. The refutation consists in arguing that the social sciences are not values-free for one or more of the following reasons: (1) Social scientists are affected by personal and social values in their choice of problems to investigate, including their career choice of the social sciences and of particular areas within them on which to work. (2) Governments and other political agencies have long used the social sciences to further various nefarious as well as (perhaps as frequently) noble aims, often with the collaboration of leading social scientists. (3) Social scientists quite often commit errors of observation and interpretation that are due to their personal and political biases.

No one has ever denied any of these banal claims. The values-free doctrine is immune to them. It is the doctrine that one cannot establish any evaluative conclusion *within* the social sciences, that is, by using scientific data and scientific or logical inferences. It has nothing to do with the question of whether the social sciences or parts of them can be valued, misused, and distorted, events that are inevitable consequences of, and will last as long as, human plans and faults, although the extent of these abuses can be limited by vigilance and commitment. The main argument for the real values-free doctrine is sometimes expressed by saying that the proper task of the sciences is to describe the way the world is, not the way it ought to be, which sounds plausible at first hearing (until one thinks about medicine, engineering, agriculture, and so on, the practitioners of which do not hesitate to say how the world, or parts thereof, ought to be and have no difficulty in backing up those claims). A common variation on this argument is expressed by saying that science establishes facts about the world, and that one cannot legitimately infer evaluative conclusions from factual premises—"ought" claims from "is" claims—hence science cannot establish evaluative claims. These are not trivial arguments and are not in any way undermined by the pseudorefutations.

That there is in fact something wrong with the real values-free doctrine is suggested by the way in which it is often expressed in the introductory psychology or sociology class or text. Even if not summed up in so many words, this position can be quite well expressed as "evaluative conclusions cannot be established by any legitimate scientific process," which is, of course, self-refutatory since it is an evaluative conclusion. The smell of fish increases if one looks at almost any scientific paper, which is likely to contain a great many evaluative conclusions, for example, about the relative merit of prior contributions to the literature, the quality of data from various sources, the merits of various experimental designs and interpretations. Under challenge, these conclusions are supported by factual and value (and definitional) premises, and the value premises turn out to be not arbitrary expressions of taste but instead perfectly defensible and actively defended positions. They are usually derived from facts combined with plausible definitions of various kinds of scientific entities.[6]

Exactly the same type of inference is used by *Consumer Reports* to establish its evaluative conclusions from its experimental evidence (by using implicit definitions of, for example, washing machines). And the same type of argument is used by values-free social scientists when grading their students or the papers that they read for scientific journals. Of course, it can also be used to establish the merit of an education or social program.

So there was a key logical blunder in the argument on which the values-free doctrine was built: the blunder of supposing that evaluative statements were all essentially arbitrary, like expressions of taste or preference, when in fact many of them have the solid status of derivations from facts and definitions. But the blunder had nothing to do with the ones listed in the pseudorefutations, and it points in a quite different direction. It suggests—as already articulated in the annals of scientific method—that we still do a poor job of spelling out and justifying our logical presuppositions, inferences, and conceptual definitions when we are doing science, or education about science. This job is something we should also do better when we are evaluating efforts to do or educate about science.[7]

People who read this suggested refutation of the values-free doctrine sometimes react by saying, "Oh, but of course no one ever denied there are *scientific* evaluative claims within science. They're sound enough because they can be translated into factual claims about outcomes of various kinds.

That wasn't the point of the values-free doctrine. It was saying that you can't establish *ethical or social* values within science." Looking at the arguments given for the doctrine, however, we can see that they claim to prove that one cannot establish *any* evaluative claims from factual and definitional premises (excluding premises that beg the question), and those arguments are refuted by the examples given. But let us ignore this point. If there is a way to establish scientific evaluative claims (for example, by translating them into factual claims about outcomes), then there are plenty of well-founded scientific evaluative claims, and the only remaining question is why anyone should think such claims cannot be made about social or education programs. If one can do the translation trick in science, why not in product evaluation? And if there, why not in program evaluation?

Of course, it is not possible literally to translate the scientific evaluative claims into descriptive language, any more than one can literally translate statements about theoretical entities into observation language. But one can more or less boil them down to sound inferences from factual and definitional premises, which is, more or less, what was meant. But then, of course, one can do the same with evaluations in other fields, including program evaluation, and often more easily.

Good scientists have long argued rationally about the merits of various ways to teach science, and thus about science curricula and pedagogy, the combination of which make up one kind of program. Such arguments bring in appeals to the purpose of science education and to why some conceptions of such purposes are unsound, others sound, why some approaches to teaching certain subject matter are better than others, and so on. So here we have scientists making and arguing rationally for social and educational value claims about the merits of programs. What is left to concede about the defeat of the values-free doctrine?

Perhaps the last-ditch stand concerns the question of whether ethics can be given a factual-cum-definitional basis. This turns out not to be too hard, once one gets down to it, as the utilitarians sensed, although they did not avoid all the traps in doing it, mainly because they lacked some parts of the more recent and essential "soft logic." These days, it is not too hard to spell out the process. Perhaps the easiest way to see that it is possible is to ask oneself whether there are any arguments for a just system of law. If there are, then they can be readily extended to provide arguments for the internalization of respect for just laws and the rights that they embody. These arguments show that valuing of such rights is justified, and such rights include most of the usual moral rights of citizens. So there are good reasons for ethical systems (see Scriven, 1966).

However, even if we do not venture into such a scandalously extreme position as arguing that ethics can be shown to be a rational policy, there is another way to demonstrate difficulties with the residual version of the values-free doctrine that claims only the impossibility of giving scientific support for social values. Consider, for example, the question of whether there are sound arguments for democracy as a form of government. Social scientists—political scientists, in this case—were forbidden, by the zeitgeist, to discuss such a question, which was relegated to political philosophy. However, there were one or two renegades who thought (along with most citizens) that there were good commonsense grounds for supposing that at least a modest case can be made for democracy. Social scientists are nowadays able to strengthen the case by appeal to decision theory, game theory, empirical studies of the failures of other forms of government, and political history. If such arguments can be made, then evaluative conclusions about social institutions can be drawn from factual premises in a non-question-begging way. Of course, the factual premises include facts about what people value, in the sense of prefer, but those are simply parameters defining the problem, not question-begging assertions about what is best or right.

Despite these cracks in the pedestal, it appears that the vast majority of social scientists maintained lip service to their version of the values-free doctrine for at least two-thirds of this century, and they probably continue to do so. When the big evaluation contracts came up for bidding in the mid to late 1960s, social scientists obviously had many of the relevant skills in testing, interviewing, and survey work; but a bystander might wonder how they could take on evaluation contracts without violating the metascientific taboo on evaluation. No problem: There was the weak decision support position and the relativistic position ready to provide them with absolution (the expression seems appropriate). Within a few years, there were three more "values-free approaches to program evaluation," dressed in the scientific robes of ethnography, sociology, and deconstructionism, to compete with the strong decision support approach.

The good news was that at last we had social scientists doing something in the area of social program evaluation. Even if it was very few of them doing very little, it was a toe in the water. The bad news was that it took two-thirds of this century for even these few to get a toe in the water, and that when they did, the way in which they did it was crippled and distorted to prevent it from violating a misconceived philosophical dogma; the distortion was serious enough to prevent them from paying attention to the worst problems of society.[8] Although there were some apparently plausible arguments for this doctrine, it was totally and obviously inconsistent with their own practice, even when they claimed to be doing purely empirical research. The plausible arguments should have been examined more carefully; their continued acceptance suggests that they supported a view more comfortable than its alternative, a view that kept the ivory tower insulated from the pains and perils of the real world. That was, after all, Weber's original argument for the doctrine of values-free social science when he introduced it, before it was elevated to the status of a religious dogma, complete with bad theology.

Society paid a terrible price for this self-indulgence, a policy that kept the social sciences out of the kitchen because of its heat. It took renegades to uncover, very late in the day, the true facts about the extent of poverty and illiteracy in our own society, about the extent of corruption in our political process, about the extent of bias in education, personnel evaluation, and public practice. The uncovering of ills of this kind was seen as value-laden research and hence taboo by the standards of the profession (although in fact it could have been undertaken in a relativistic framework).

Even science itself paid a terrible price for the values taboo. Not only was the funding of research done imperfectly because no one was willing to look scientifically at the validity of the peer review process (despite clear indications that it was flawed), not only was personnel evaluation done shoddily (weakening the research groups and faculties), but science education was done shoddily because evaluation of the efforts in that field was treated as something other than a standard part of any scientific activity.

The irony of this dismissal of many useful kinds of evaluation was not only that it was done by those who failed to notice that they were violating the (invalid) taboo throughout their scientific work, but also that doing it involved abandonment of two valid and vital precepts of science and all other academic disciplines. First, science is committed to the idea that a scientist's conclusions must, wherever possible, be supported by externally accessible evidence and argument. Yet, when scientists started running science education projects, few were ever evaluated in a way that met that standard, which, of course, required competent external evaluation and replication.[9] Second, the ideal of science as cumulative knowledge requires that validated results be published so that others can learn from them. There is no reason to suppose that the results of experiments in science education are any different from results in any other part of science. But since the science education projects were rarely evaluated in a way that made them entries in the validated results stakes, we learned little from them; hence fashion holds sway, and progress is fragile or illusory rather than cumulative.

It is now time to look in more detail at the approaches that provided the first tiny taste of the forbidden fruit of evaluation in the 1960s.

Thesis 1: Program evaluation is not a determination of goal attainment

The most obvious way to do evaluation without actually making any evaluative statements of our own is to restrict ourselves to factual claims about what happened and measure these results against our clients' standards of value. The relevant type of conclusion from this kind of study is

"The program met/did not meet its goals, to such and such a degree and in such and such respects." Since the early program evaluations were commissioned by managers—Congress or the agencies—who had already decided that the goals of the program were good, this kind of conclusion was just what they wanted to know. They did not need the evaluator to question the goals. So this relativistic approach passed quite successfully as evaluation, until a few critics started raising questions about the justification or importance of the goals. Obviously, they were not persuaded that success in meeting those goals was proof of merit in the program. Obviously, too, what they were doing was also program evaluation. So began the process of discovering chinks in the armor of the first and most primitive model of values-free program evaluation, the approach that maintained that evaluation is simply a determination of the success of a program in meeting its goals. In the course of refuting this approach, I call on much that has been laid out in the introduction and in turn lay the groundwork for many of the corollaries expressed in later theses.

Project Monitoring. Project monitoring is an important management support task that bears some relation to program evaluation. Monitoring is often described as checking to see that projects, or programs, are "on-time, on-task, and on-budget," which is close to evaluation according to the discrepancy model, one of the relativistic values-free approaches.[10] There is usually also a check that mandated guidelines for all programs, for example, those that bear on equal employment, continue to be met; the term *compliance monitoring* is often used to indicate attention to that kind of consideration.

For reasons of time, monitoring is normally done in a relatively passive way by the project officer, who used to be called the project monitor, through perusal of project reports and other documents, sometimes but not always combined with visits to the project site. Monitoring is an essential and appropriate part of the accountability efforts of federal agencies. It does not involve second-guessing of the goals of the project or program and thus focuses on (apparent) progress toward those goals, without commitment to their rightness or wrongness. If described as program evaluation, this feature would place it in the relativistic camp. The check on compliance can even be phrased in relativistic terms, as a comment about meeting existing legal requirements on procedures. It would be a further step, and one that goes beyond relativism, to conclude that the project is proceeding unethically because of its violation of the regulations; and project monitors do have to make that call from time to time.

Monitoring in the superficial way allowed by time constraints does not constitute a serious effort at evaluation, because the process of determining whether a project has achieved its goals requires more than passive investigation by the monitor. A passive, for example, "read-all-documents," investigation by a specialist in the project's area is a significant step toward stronger monitoring. But unless the funding agency, the program, or the project commissions a serious external evaluation, reliance on standard documentation is completely inadequate as a basis for determining whether the goals have been reached.

There are many other key questions that an evaluator must ask that are not part of the standard monitor's charge. Moreover, the monitor's tasks may also include the setting up or monitoring of external evaluations of projects or programs, ranging from mere visits by experts to full-scale evaluations by external evaluators. These evaluations tend to be goal-oriented, since that is the orientation of the monitor and the monitor's supervisors. But because of their extra resources, they are, typically, actively investigative rather than passively analytical and come nearer to determining whether the goals have been attained, to what extent, and in what respects, perhaps even at what real cost. On the way to this determination, they normally involve activities that disturb the project more than the monitor's activity, especially if interim results are communicated to the project while it is ongoing. This increased effect is not all bad; in fact, it is one reason that external formative evaluations are commissioned, as it is often clear that some such interaction is called for.

A key problem for monitors is conflict of interest. The logic of their situation forces them to represent the project back at the agency headquarters, and, indeed, there is a sense in which this is part of their duties. But this role, and the constant interaction with the project staff, erodes their independence across a year or less—sometimes across one lunch table—so the monitor cannot always be counted on for an independent view. Hence external evaluators are crucial on important projects. When the same person is used to monitor the evaluation contract for these external evaluators and the project being evaluated, this conflict of interest has at times led to pressure on the evaluator to make the project look good. There are ways to control this problem, as discussed in Chapter Six of this volume.

Proto-Evaluation. This investigatory extension of monitoring can, if done thoroughly, be thought of as "proto-evaluation," a kind of zero-order case of evaluation. Its strengths are that it is external, that is, the investigator is usually less ego-involved with the program than is the monitor (partly because the investigator has no duty to represent the project to the agency); it puts a much stronger emphasis on outcomes rather than process, in comparison to monitoring; it is investigative rather than passive; and it normally involves special expertise tailored to the subject matter or type of project, as well as to the type of investigation. If we want to think of it as a primitive species of program evaluation, then we might use the term *goal achievement evaluation:* It is a kind of program evaluation in which success or failure is measured essentially by reference to the goals of the program. The reports from such evaluations do not endorse or reject the goals and hence are relativistic in the same way as the reports from the passive monitor; and they also omit many other dimensions of true program evaluation. Nevertheless, in many human services areas—notably, public health and criminal justice—this approach is still thought of by most practitioners as what evaluation really is; this is what their graduate students are taught; and many texts still define program evaluation in this way. The definition often identifies the following steps:

1. Determine the goals of the program from program documents or personnel.
2. Convert these into measurable objectives.
3. Find or construct tests that measure these objectives.
4. Run the tests on an appropriate sample of the target population.
5. Use data synthesis techniques to amalgamate the results in order to determine whether or to what extent the program met its goals.
6. Report the program evaluation results in terms of the program's success in meeting its goals.

The proto-evaluator usually casts a glance around for side effects. But the task of handling these effects, once they have been identified, turns out to be quite a tricky business if the only standards of value are the goals of the program, since side effects are by definition not going to rack up points on those scales of merit (see Thesis 4).

Contracts let to do this kind of evaluation are usually referred to as evaluation contracts. True program evaluation, however, involves considerably more—and can involve less—than this approach, and it is considerably more important, not only to society as a whole but also to an agency's agenda. In particular, it must go beyond acceptance of the goals into evaluation of them, it must consider costs and comparisons, and it sometimes benefits from ignoring the goals entirely, except in an appendix to the evaluation report.

The idea of the evaluator critiquing the goals may seem at first to be counterintuitive, since Congress or the executive branch has mandated that the program be done in order to meet goals that those higher powers perceive as important. But the difference between the role of the monitor or proto-evaluator and the role of the serious evaluator is radical. In the role of monitoring, this accepting attitude toward the goals is not only defensible but mandatory; and the task of monitoring is entirely proper. There is no suggestion here that it be abandoned in favor of something else; the suggestion is that it needs to be supplemented by a more serious kind of evaluation, indeed by something considerably more extensive than proto-evaluation or goal achievement evaluation.

Management-Oriented Versus Consumer-Oriented Models of Evaluation. Monitoring and the somewhat-more-than-monitoring that I have been calling proto-evaluation or goal achievement evaluation tell the program manager what he or she needs to know about the progress of the program toward its goals, but they do a severely limited job for the recipient, the taxpayer, the citizen, and those concerned with the welfare of program impactees. (There is an indirect payoff to the consumer since goal achievement evaluation is part of good management practices if done with skill and if its results are implemented.) These parties need something more like a consumer model of evaluation. A demonstration of why such a model is very different should create a presumption that federal and state agencies *also* need to do evaluations that are more consumer-oriented, since the agencies are in some sense the instruments of government, and government in a democracy is in some sense an agency of the people. However, there are also more direct reasons, which are discussed later, for the agency to take a point of view on program evaluation that transcends a goal achievement approach.

Most consumer or taxpayer groups have little interest in whether a program meets its goals as such, only in whether it does something that needs doing, whether the cost is reasonable, and whether it does it better than alternative ways of doing it. And, from their point of view, the standards for judging whether it does the job well or better must include standards of equity and environmental responsibility, not just short-term economy. None of these issues is addressed by goal achievement evaluation, and only their surface is scratched by compliance monitoring.

Since every employee of an agency wears a consumer's hat when not at work, it is easy enough for them to understand the consumer orientation. When did anyone buying a bicycle or a stove ever ask the salesperson for the goals of the design group at the manufacturer's plant? They try the product out to see how well it serves their needs, look at competitive products, and consider or dicker on the price. That is, they look at comparative cost-effectiveness in meeting the needs of the consumer. Maybe they also avoid crossing picket lines to make the purchase; maybe they also give some credit if the product is made in the United States and check whether there are any Environmental Protection Agency suits pending against the manufacturer—all of which puts an element of ethics in the filter. That is what product evaluation looks like. And done as well as the informed individual does it using readily available product evaluations, it is a very powerful way to obtain highly cost-effective benefits. It does not involve any checking on progress toward goals.

Why should program evaluation be essentially different? After all, programs are simply ways of getting things done, just as artifacts are devices for getting things done: Both can be evaluated quite thoroughly with a little effort. There are plenty of programs around, now or in the past, in schools, hospitals, and businesses, whose success or failure and merit or worth have been clearly established in particular contexts. Surely it is a mistake to say that it is inappropriate for program evaluation to be looking for the truth about the merit or worth of a program. But that is the position of all but the first of the six common approaches identified earlier. Guba and Lincoln (1989, pp. 7–8) put it most strongly: "We do not treat evaluation as a scientific process . . . evaluation outcomes are not descriptions of the 'way things really are' or 'really work' or of some 'true' state of affairs." It seems more plausible to say that the merit or worth of things and people is part of what they are really like, of what is true about them, just as much as their popularity, their cost of upkeep, or their capabilities and potential, and that we are fully conversant with the process of determining those properties. Certainly, merit and worth vary with the context, but then so also do cost and durability, the most practical of considerations. We know how to handle that variation, and we still regard cost and durability as properties of things. Merit and worth are also contextual properties of things and people.

Program Evaluation Versus Product Evaluation. I have already mentioned two alleged differences between programs and products: complexity and political considerations. Here, I quickly summarize the whole family of such suggestions and the replies to them. The usual comments are as follows: "Surely programs are essentially different from products. They are more complex, more amorphous, constantly changing, and political footballs. Moreover, their goals are less clear; and how can one criticize their goals except from one's own point of view, which is no more provably the right view?"

Programs are not all complex, and none is clearly more complex than big artifacts such as the Stealth bomber or massively parallel computers, with more than a billion components. In any case, why should "more complex" mean any more than that the evaluation will cost more and take more expertise? After all, it is more complex to determine the world's population than a town's population, more difficult to determine the temperature of the interior of the sun than that of the interior of one's own house—so we use experts to do the more difficult tasks. Is the gap any bigger in dealing with programs?

True, programs are often amorphous, fuzzy around the edges and hard to define, but so also, when we come to evaluate them, are highways, insecticides, and atomic power plants, and those are the targets of technology assessment—the general version of product evaluation. The Office of Technology Assessment does this job very well and without violating scientific standards.

True, programs change substantially, within limits. But that is true of many things that we are used to evaluating, such as the uses of a computer, the structure and health of corporations, the quality of a student's writing, the abilities of a child, and investment portfolios.

Political footballs? Remember the battery additive AD-X2, the supercollider, the interstate highway system, and the space station, among many other examples.

The goals of programs are often not transparent, but then it is not so easy to identify the goals of the superconducting supercollider or of a rental car. Products do not have goals, and that should remind us that evaluation does not need goals. Goals are only essential for planning and running the production process for products, and for running programs. Evaluation is another matter.

Finally, with respect to the supposed substitution of one's own values for the program's values, it is important to remember that in evaluating the goals of programs, we appeal to needs assessments done on the targeted population, to serious cost analysis, to internal and external logical consistency, to research on what is possible, and to legal and ethical considerations, among other considerations, but never to our own values. These are simply the generalization of the considerations that we use in evaluating products for our own use. In a good evaluation of a program impacting people other than the evaluator, it should be impossible to identify the values of the evaluator.

So none of these suggestions provides any serious reason to think that the process of program evaluation should be regarded as essentially different from the evaluation of products, technologies, real estate, insurance companies, nursing homes, and so on—the things that we are all used to seeing evaluated. There is no need to abandon the product evaluation paradigm, which is the best available "consumer model" for program evaluation. The worst that can be said is that program evaluation is perhaps more often hard to do and more complex. But it is also sometimes simpler (see Thesis 17).

It is obvious that the best consumer-oriented product evaluation is done by highly independent evaluators, and the same is equally desirable for consumer-oriented approaches to program evaluation.[11] This means avoiding the use of evaluators who benefit in any way from making the program look good, or making a program instigator or manager look good. This constraint rules out the use of the program's own staff, the monitor, and other funding agency staff, and it requires considerable care in the choice of external evaluators (see Thesis 27). Nevertheless, to the extent that an agency represents, or wishes to represent, or is intended to represent, the interests of those citizens who pay the bill and want to know if the money was well spent or wasted, and those who have or care about the needs that the program is intended to fulfill, it seems clear that this is the kind of approach that the agency should make an effort to implement. It is this point of view, or type of approach, that generates program evaluation rather than program monitoring or proto-evaluation. If this argument is accepted, there is no need to contrast management models with consumer models; a good management model can and should include both elements. When it does so, it is entitled to be called evaluation.

There is another way to approach the conclusion that the agency has an obligation to look at programs in terms of the consumer's point of view. It begins by noting that an agency can never avoid responsibility for the programs that it administers by saying that it was ordered to implement them and hence has no responsibility to evaluate them. Even the modern conventions of war hold soldiers responsible for evaluating the actions that they are commanded to perform, to the extent possible in the heat of battle, and they are accountable for performing those actions if they violate fundamental human rights. Congress is not a one-party body, and at least the minority party holds agencies fully responsible for watchful implementation of the programs that they administer, even though they were ordered to implement them. For at least this reason, the U.S. offices of the inspectors general and the General Accounting Office do full-spectrum evaluations, not simply routine checks to see if monitoring occurred and was done competently.

So the message is clear: Even an agency, which does not originate legislation, has to look beyond monitoring and mere goal achievement evaluation. External evaluation advisers and contractors are more clearly committed to their jobs if they are hired to do more than proactive monitoring. If they are hired to do any serious kind of evaluation, or if they have high professional standards even though they were only hired for goal achievement monitoring, they must care that the interests of all, not just those of the present administration and Congress, are preserved. And, of course, they are more subject to liability suits.

These are reasons for only applying the term evaluation to approaches that include serious attention to the consumer's viewpoint. Still, why not just say that the management approach and the consumer approach are two different approaches to evaluation? After all, goal achievement evaluation was widely described, even among evaluators, as one model of evaluation—the discrepancy model—and it is listed as such in many taxonomies of models of evaluation. The argument here is that when one comes to look in detail at what this approach omits, as we do next, and when one comes to ask what the evaluator can reasonably be expected to cover, it becomes clear that it is really only an extension of monitoring, and the best we can possibly call it is proto-evaluation. Even when done professionally and externally, it is no more than a step or two on the twelve-step path toward something that can properly be called evaluation.

Missing Factor 1: Side Effects. Whether or not programs do what they are supposed to do, they often produce other effects, unanticipated or unemphasized, and it is surely a program administrator's responsibility to find out what these are and how important they are. They may be very serious: In the case of the Food and Drug Administration, whose business is product evaluation, the side-effect search is by far the greater part of their investigatory efforts. It is not often that a manufacturer submits a pharmaceutical for review that does not achieve its intended effects, at least to a substantial degree. The issue is nearly always whether and to what extent it has undesirable side effects.

The monitoring of progress toward achieving program goals does not usually or necessarily involve an active search for side effects. Indeed, identification of side effects in any systematic way is often difficult because those who know the program well quickly develop tunnel vision, their attention becomes focused on what they are looking for and hoping to find. External evaluators tend to be better at identifying side effects simply because they have fresh eyes, although sometimes a new internal staff member or an exchange staff member can be used with great success.

For an external evaluator, or for a new staff person, the so-called goal-free approach to program evaluation has the special merit of avoiding much of the cueing toward goals that occurs when an evaluator is exposed to program documents and goal-directed personnel. It may be the best methodology for identifying side effects. What does this mean in practice? Just that before new staffers are briefed on the program, they should be sent out to the field to report on what they see at a site where the program is being delivered, and on what they hear from recipients there, without talking to service providers. This is a good training practice and tests their capacity for uncued observation, and it often provides crucial insights to the program administrator.[12]

Now, side effects not only have to be sought but also have to be evaluated as serious or trivial, fatal or fortunate. How does one decide on the importance, or even on the merit, of side effects? This evaluation cannot be done by reference to the only standards of value that the values-free social scientist came in with—those contained in the goals of a program—because the side effects are by definition irrelevant to the goals, that is, they are of zero value if the goals are the only standards of value.

The answer is to look at how the side effects bear on the needs, and sometimes on the rights, of those on whom they are inflicted or bestowed. To use these needs as standards of merit, we have to do or find a current needs assessment—something not covered in the monitoring model and something that may entail a considerable cost. As discussed in a moment, there is another reason why we have to have the results of a needs assessment, arising from another dimension of program evaluation not covered by the monitoring approach. Additionally, there are other standards of value, such as legal, ethical, and environmental standards, that must be consulted in evaluating side effects.

There is a special kind of side effect that probably deserves its own name. We might call it *side impact,* or the impact of a program on populations that were not targeted. The side-impacted group may well receive exactly the intended effects, or else quite different effects. The identification of side impacts requires a different kind of investigation from a side-effect search because it requires the investigator to find another population, not just other effects on the same population. The two factors interact, of course; one needs a four-cell study in which one can locate intended and unintended effects on targeted and nontargeted impactees. Each cell may contain unique elements. Thus, in conventional monitoring and goal achievement evaluation, one looks to see if the target group has been reached and the intended effects produced. Considering side impacts, one looks to see who else is affected, and what the effects were, intended or otherwise, on them as well as on the target group. In any case, the monitor, the internal evaluator, and any external formative evaluators are the early-warning system for the decision maker, and they should be searching conscientiously for these unintended or incidental effects—and impactees—since these factors may determine the fate of the program.

Missing Factor 2: Overruns and Shortfalls. The problem of assessing the importance of overruns and shortfalls along the goal dimensions is methodologically related to the problem of dealing with side effects. (I am using the terms overruns and shortfalls to refer to effect size, not to costs.) In the real world, it is very rare for specific goals and specific targeted populations to be exactly reached. What counts as a significant shortfall or overrun, or a significant effect on a side-impacted group? If we just use the goals as standards, all we can say is that a shortfall is a failure and an overrun a success (and analogously with side impacts). But shortfalls may be brilliant successes, because it took brilliance to get that close to what were excessively ambitious goals; and big overruns may be trivial, because the goals were trivial (even if there are no side effects and side impacts). As with side effects and side impacts, we have to turn to the needs assessment (and other relevant values) in order to deal with these phenomena. And once we have a needs assessment, the question arises of whether we should be using goal achievement standards at all. We can replace them by using the needs from the needs assessment as the criteria of merit for *all* effects, whether intended or not, whether they represent shortfalls or overruns (or side effects and side impacts) or precisely the intended effects. That is what makes goal-free evaluation possible. It is not criteria-free; it is needs-based instead of goal-based. Moreover, there is another key role for the needs assessment; and if we stay with any type of goal-based evaluation, even if it is much more sophisticated than mere goal achievement evaluation, we will have to use the needs assessment in this role—so why not switch to using it as the only standard of merit and worth? One answer is that we may want to add a comment about the extent to which the goals were met, as a service to the manager, if the manager is one of the clients. But that turns out not to be as easy as it sounds. And it is an expensive path, not a free add-on to the needs assessment, which cannot be avoided in any case.

Missing Factor 3: Problems with Goals. So far, I have been addressing the problem of dealing with results that are not exactly what was intended.

But, clearly, there may be problems about the goals themselves, for example, about their relevance or adequacy for the target population, or about the justification for targeting that population. Hence there may be problems about the results even if they are exactly as intended. The main two reasons why even the agency monitor and any serious program evaluator employed by the agency should do some checking on the appropriateness of goals are the agency's ultimate obligation to the consumer and the need to be prepared for a seriously negative summative evaluation—the early warning role of the evaluator. These reasons also explain why evaluators who are employed by anyone besides the funding agency, for example, an oversight agency, a consumer group, or the media, or who are working on a research project must look critically at goals. Foremost, there are problems that may arise about the goals, even if they were originally based on a good needs assessment.

Coping with Changes. Priorities and personnel are constantly changing at the legislative as well as the recipient levels, sometimes dramatically, and the wish or need to reconsider a program often arises. Hence there is a need to provide, or to obtain, information not only about the performance of a program but also about its current payoff on the needs at which it was originally targeted, the continued importance of those needs, and the changes in knowledge about those needs. Many years often pass between the invention of a particular program, especially a large program, and the point when a major evaluation of it begins. In between, the enabling legislation is constructed and passed; the program is set up, developed, and distributed; and all the while it is modified via running changes that turn out to be required by practical considerations not foreseen when the program was designed. The original needs assessment, even if competent, is often outdated during this period.

There are several different reasons for these changes, other than the vicissitudes of Washington politics. There are often changes in the availability of other services aimed at meeting the same generic needs, sometimes because of other federal efforts and sometimes because of state or private foundation efforts; such changes can reduce or marginalize the need for a specific program. The needs of the target population can change through learning or maturation, for example, basic consciousness-raising seminars for college women are now hardly the priority that they once were. The size of the target population may change substantially, partly because of the success of the target program and other programs, making the program as originally conceived a less than optimal way of dealing with the recipients. Our knowledge of the best way to meet given needs may change substantially, a common situation in the intercultural and computer education scene, for example. The fundamental political presuppositions on which the original needs analysis was based may change, for example, when other minorities are recognized as having a legitimate claim to attention. A consideration that is specific to the education area is that the subject matter knowledge in a field may change, which can change the need for a particular package of curriculum materials. Finally, new needs may emerge as new vocations emerge or new weaknesses in the preparation for other vocations emerge. For all of these reasons, the goals of a program are not immune to reassessment, and the evaluator must gather the data needed to provide a running reassessment.

Correcting Start-Up Mistakes. Next, there is the problem of goals that were based on poor needs assessment in the first place. In the course of doing a new needs assessment, to cover the possibility that needs have changed, it frequently becomes clear and should be recorded (perhaps rather tactfully) that the original goals were not well matched to the needs. This should be done for at least four reasons: accountability, historical accuracy, facilitation of learning, and professionalism. An evaluator is not doing an acceptable job in reporting a program as successful on the grounds that it met needs that were never significant (but only thought to be so, or only thought to be politically attractive at the time).

Sometimes these basic errors about the needs assessment that led to the creation of a program require a major rethinking of all programs in an area. For example, in the late 1950s and early 1960s, there was serious criticism of K–12 social studies curricula because they were explicitly intended— virtually by indoctrination rather than ratiocination—to inculcate students with existing social norms (which did not include equal rights for minorities and women).

The most notable errors in goal setting involve unrealistically high goals (for example, that students in this country will score at the top of the international science and math comparisons by the year 2000) and unnecessarily low ones (for example, that students in this country will improve their ranking in the same comparisons by the same date). These are usually not just random but rather motivated errors. Goals are often set unrealistically high because this practice has rhetorical appeal and, as long as they are to be met at a time when the administration setting them will no longer be around, there is little downside risk. The practice of setting goals low is the best way to ensure they will be met without undue effort and is the besetting sin of education programs in which teachers or trainers of teachers are the principal standard setters. This bias toward low-setting is so widespread as to constitute an overwhelming reason not to accept goals as reasonable standards of merit, even if there are no other reasons to reject them. When goals are complicated or spelled out in detail, they also turn out, quite frequently, to contain internal inconsistencies, or inconsistencies with known facts. More frequently, there are ethical or legal problems with them. Goals make a very poor given.

Defending Goals. The validity of goals is thus ephemeral and needs revalidation. If criticisms are to be met, the program evaluator needs to be able to produce evidence of the relevance and importance of the goals. So the other side of the previous point is that a new needs assessment, because more current or more thorough, or a reanalysis of the old assessment can sometimes provide a better defense of the goals than is possible by merely quoting the original needs assessment.

Avoiding Goals. The topic here has been about how one has to do more than use the goals of a program when looking for standards by which to value the outcomes—or, for that matter, the process—of a program. But it is often worth considering whether one should do less, that is, whether there are serious costs involved in even using goals in program evaluation.

The first problem is the seriously biasing effect on the evaluator of knowing the goals of a program; they cue the evaluator toward seeing them in the effects. The second is that thorough determination of the goals of a program is a very complex and costly process. It often turns out to be extremely difficult to answer the question, What *are* the goals of the program? Should we be using the goals of the committee originating the legislation? Or the goals actually incorporated in the language of the legislation (which often incorrectly interprets the intent of the committee, as the General Accounting Office has discovered)? The goals of the current program director? The goals of the site managers, often substantially modified in the light of reality, without anyone mentioning this "upstairs"? The goals of the workers, often representing a further modification?

Then there is the problem of deciding whether to use the implicit goals of these players, those that they believe to be their own; or the ones that they are prepared to endorse publicly ("latent" versus "manifest" goals in the language of the social anthropologist). There is also the problem of inconsistency, both within one source and across sources. Should we try to use only the common elements in the goals? Should we try to arbitrate the disagreements? What about goals that plainly rest on factual assumptions that turn out to be false? To think carefully about these problems in terms of evaluation design is to recognize another, very attractive reason for using goal-free methodology—it avoids this mess.

The goal-free approach is "the path less taken" in program (and perhaps in policy) evaluation, but not in product evaluation.[13] It requires some development of linguistic sensitivities, since goals are often built into the way in which we talk about programs, and, like sexist language, it takes a while to learn how to purge oneself of that. For example, programs are often thought of in terms of being successful or effective. But one cannot be successful without having aimed at something, and the usual way we talk about effectiveness also implies that there were goals to be attained. This is managerial talk (often used by us in discussing our own projects), not an essential part of the minimalist vocabulary of evaluation, and in fact of limited interest from the point of view of taxpayers or recipients when talking about someone else's program. From the point of view of such consumers, a different terminology is appropriate. Programs are *valuable* to a greater or lesser degree, *worth what they cost* to a greater or lesser degree, *beneficial* or *harmful* on balance. And they become valuable by doing what it takes to meet needs—whether or not by design—better than the alternatives and with fewer bad outcomes. Goals are part of the language of intentions, and it is the road to hell that is paved with good intentions. The road to the other place is paved with good achievements.

Needs Assessment Instead of Goal Identification. A good deal has been laid on the needs assessment in this discussion, and one should not act as if doing this kind of assessment is a trivial matter by comparison with identification of goals. In much of the literature, needs assessment *is* trivialized, since needs are defined as the gap between ideals and the status quo. If one makes the further mistake of thinking that people are reliable judges of what is ideal for them, this suggests that one can reduce the needs assessment process to a survey of what the impacted population thinks is required in order to achieve their ideals. In fact, surveys of this kind are close to being mere "wants assessments" and have little to do with needs. Needs are not the gap between the status quo and an ideal state but rather the gap between nothing and what is required to stave off malfunction, for example, the amount of vitamin C that we *need* to prevent scurvy and other hypovitaminotic conditions. Needs assessments require careful study of where malfunction occurs, and then of the causal tree that leads to it, in order to determine what could have avoided the malfunction that is under the control of the service provider.

A simple example is the discovery that employers discard many job applications that they believe show signs of illiteracy, and that this elimination can be avoided by targeted remedial literacy instruction in the high school. Once we know this, we do not need to do a new needs assessment for each evaluation of high school literacy catch-up classes. In many other evaluations, the needs assessment can rely on prior research. Quite often, however, an intelligent analytical needs assessment has to be done, especially when side effects and side impacts turn up that must be evaluated by relating them to needs.

Needs Are Not Enough. Prior reference has been made to "relevant needs assessment," but, more precisely, a needs assessment is not enough for comprehensive goal and side-effect evaluation. We need to review all relevant values, or standards of value, that bear on the goals, including, for example, scientific findings, futurist projections, and professional, ethical, logical, legal, and environmental standards—and sometimes just plain preferences (when no needs override them). In most actual cases, once the needs assessment is done, it is only a matter of an hour or two more to run down and apply these values. In recent times, the term *needs assessment* has often been extended to include a review of all relevant values. Some of these considerations involve so-called absolute values.

Missing Factor 3: Absolute Values. Absolute values, as the term is used here, are simply values that transcend practical concerns. In a particular case, for example, the evaluation of a school computer laboratory, it may be a practical value that the laboratory occupies minimal space or costs less than $1,000 per station. But the safety requirements are "absolute," that is, one cannot risk having students get severe electrical shocks. The "cannot" here refers to ethical constraints, and not just to liability suits; the "absolute" does not mean that there are no circumstances in which the requirement can be overridden, only that it takes other absolute values to override it, not practical values (although there are limit cases, even then). Similarly, in teaching in the laboratory, it is a practical requirement to cover the state-mandated curriculum, but it is an absolute requirement to avoid racial slurs.

There is little reference to absolute values in the standard texts on program evaluation. The leading text does not even have one index entry for ethics. While the social scientists were willing to do goal achievement evaluation, they were not going to make any direct value claims and were doubly opposed to getting into the business of making ethical judgments concerning programs. In fact, they avoided getting into the business of making legal judgments. But that attitude is from the ivory tower. In reality, there is probably no evaluator who would argue for leaving out of an evaluation report the discovery that the program manager is stealing from the till, sexually harassing the office staff, running an illegal book in the office, or refusing to promote clearly superior minority staff members. While there are plenty of problems of correctly interpreting the code of ethics that we have built into this society and its laws, there are also plenty of cases where we are not in the least doubt that something morally improper—or laudatory—has occurred. It is truly unethical to leave ethics out of program evaluation, a fact well recognized in the work of a number of professional associations (see Joint Committee on Standards for Educational Evaluation, 1980).

One can hardly argue that only egregious breaches of ethical standards are important, any more than one can argue that known breaches of ethical standards should not be mentioned in an evaluation report. It follows that the evaluator often needs at least some skill in applied ethics, and at least some basic training in legal standards in order to avoid nasty suits for defamation. But it seems likely that a defense of truth would suffice, and, presumably, evaluators are in a position to make that defense about the conclusions included in their reports. As discussed under Thesis 23, there are sometimes better ways to handle ethical errors than to put them in a written report.

There is an ancillary role of ethics in program evaluation that concerns issues of professional ethics for the evaluator. This role is given some attention in Cronbach and others (1980, pp. 198–207). *Standards for*

Evaluations of Educational Programs (Joint Committee on Standards for Educational Evaluation, 1980) is not, however, restricted to that concern.

Of course, ethics is not the only source of absolute standards. People in the fields of science, mathematics, engineering, and technology (SMET) feel most comfortable with the standards of truth, scientific truth in particular. The advisory committees from federal agencies in these areas would never allow curriculum materials to be used if they presented conclusions that were clearly inconsistent with the best current views in these fields.[14] But that kind of truth is often included in the goals of a program, and I am listing here the reasons why monitoring or measuring against goals is not enough for the program evaluator. So the more important cases for this argument are cases where one must appeal to ethical standards, legal standards, fiscal standards, logical standards, and, perhaps, ecological standards, as well as the standards of any other discipline (for example, accounting) that is incidentally involved in the management or content of a program.

Apart from these absolute standards, which are in one way secondary to the main dimension for judging education programs even though they can be overriding, there are also absolute standards of merit in the main dimension of education programs, student learning. In the grading of student work, there really are such things as correct and complete answers, and completely false or irrelevant answers, to technically sound and educationally appropriate questions. Such answers are what anchor the ends of the grading scale, and these end points refer to an important kind of absolute standard. When we see these answers, we give real grades, not conditional or relativistic grades. Analogously, there are outstanding programs for doing worthwhile tasks in SMET education that simply have to be evaluated as excellent, not just "Excellent, if you happen to think these tasks are worthwhile." (These tasks are most easily found in connection with small and well-defined areas of skills and knowledge, for example, explaining the phases of the moon.) We do not just happen to think that the programs are worthwhile, we can *show* that they are worthwhile via needs assessment. Hence the conditional clause in the conditional claim is true and the absolute conclusion follows. Knowledge cannot consist only of conditional (relativistic) claims; we need only try to imagine a science that can never make a categorical statement. And evaluation that is only conditional cannot provide us with the kind of knowledge that we need for practical purposes.

People who think that it is possible to identify some curriculum content as unsound and some student answers to examination questions as unsound should realize that they are committed to making categorical and not just conditional or relativistic value claims. Hence the burden of proof is on them to show why programs cannot also be classified as unsound, for example, if they contain large sections of unsound content and a scoring key for student answers that gives the wrong answers as correct. Apart from the kind of standards to which the term *absolute* is conventionally applied, there are standards that come close to being "categorical imperatives" of program management and hence of program evaluation, such as the need for some kind of bookkeeping and some kind of ongoing evaluation of the process and results of the program.

Missing Factor 4: Cost Analysis. Another reason why one has to go beyond monitoring or goal achievement evaluation in order to do true program evaluation is that those approaches rarely involve serious cost analysis. Most of the exceptions occur when a program has cost-effectiveness as one of its goals. Usually, monitoring is done in a context of an already settled budget, and the monitor has the task of ensuring that the project keeps within that budget. However, the budget for the project has little to do with the cost of the product, whether it is services or educational materials. In program evaluation, especially of education programs, cost is crucial. After all, almost all education goals could be quite readily achieved by the use of enough individual tutoring time, if we used highly trained expert tutors carefully matched to their pupils and the best available materials. The main reason that we bother with evaluation of school-based or museum-based or video-based instruction is that we cannot afford tutors on that scale. Everyone knows that. But if the evaluator does not do cost analysis, not everyone will know which programs or materials fall within the narrow and extremely low band of cost-feasibility for school use in this country.

We discovered very late in the game with one of the New Math curricula that millions of dollars had been sunk into a program that, once we looked at cost analysis, was completely irrelevant to 99.999 percent of our schools. That money was wasted simply because of poor early program evaluation, and, of course, incompetent program design, since this result was predictable by anyone who knew enough and was sane enough to realize that materials cost would affect dissemination.

The usual response to this point is something along the lines of, "Oh, well, okay, so we should do cost analysis." One might as well say, "Oh well, so we should make adjustments for relativistic mass changes." Cost analysis is a very sophisticated business, and it is rare to find anyone like Henry Levin who can do it at the level where it meets the demands of practical evaluation for decision making (see Levin, 1983, and Levin in McLaughlin and Phillips, 1991). Costs are not just monetary; but even monetary cost analysis in education is something far beyond the general skills of an accountant (for example, the costing of laboratories requires task-specific expertise to identify hidden costs, downtime costs, maintenance and supply costs, and so on). And often the psychological costs are far more important than the monetary costs (as in teaching heterogeneous classes). Or the space costs may be more important than the monetary costs (for example, the space needed for a dedicated computer laboratory), or the opportunity costs (for example, for an addition to the curriculum that requires something else to be eliminated), or the costs in required expertise (for example, for technology studies). If a degree of sophistication is needed to discover and measure program outcomes, including the unexpected ones, it must be just as hard to do cost analysis because costs are the input analogue of outcomes, and the unexpected costs can be just as decisive. But there is little about cost analysis in the training of most of those who are currently doing program evaluation, even in medicine where the costs are so often devastating, let alone in education (see Rossi and Freeman, 1989, for a serious discussion of cost analysis).

Cost analysis is just a neglected field, not an exceptionally difficult one. Its neglect is associated with a degree of academic prejudice against what is perceived as its dirty-hands nature. In searching for expertise on the subject in the 1970s, I was amused to find hasty disavowals of its relevance, not just by the country's leading economics departments but also by most of the top business schools. As far as I could tell, the former were setting their sights on eminence in economic theory as part of the quest for a Nobel Prize, and the latter were setting their sights on becoming economics departments. The latter aspiration brings to mind the desire of educational psychology departments to be mainline psychology departments; the former aspiration reminds one of the relation of mainline psychology departments to classical physics. Both attitudes are equally absurd, as well as irresponsible, since the applied field is at least as challenging intellectually as the more academic one (which is considerably more subject to the dictates of fashion), and the applied field has the nontrivial, if dull, advantage of being more useful.

Missing Factor 5: Comparisons. It is not enough to determine that a program meets its goals, or that it does so without bad side effects, or that it does all this at an affordable cost. The key question still remains, Could we have done better for the same (or lower) costs (or very much better at a slightly higher cost, or nearly as well for much less, and so on)? If evaluators are to be useful to consumers or policymakers, for whom the value of evaluation is usually to help them choose among alternatives, they cannot just evaluate one of the alternatives against absolute standards, that is, grade it. They must evaluate each of the important alternatives and do so using the same standards, that is, rank them. Moreover, they may well have to supplement the list of alternatives that the client has in mind when calling for the evaluation, both because the client is not always fully cognizant of the options in a particular subfield and because, as the evaluation proceeds, facts may emerge that either rule out some early runners or reveal other options as competitive alternatives. This process requires a certain kind of local expertise, which, of course, is often best obtained by using local experts to supplement whatever knowledge the evaluator may have.

Evaluators must have, or be able to get and judge for quality, this kind of local knowledge. It does not follow that they must have remedial knowledge in the field. Thus, the road tester of a car must know the competition for the car that is being evaluated in order to set reasonable standards and consider comparative cost-effectiveness. But that does not mean that he or she must have the skills of an engine designer or a suspension engineer, the skills needed in order to suggest how to remedy limitations that appear during the testing. These differences among types of local knowledge are crucial for distinguishing between evaluations and recommendations, discussed further under Thesis 7.

Does this need for comparisons mean that evaluation of one program always entails evaluation of several? Fortunately not, since many of the alternatives have already been evaluated. And sometimes the alternative is simply the no-treatment option; if it is, there will be little extra cost. Overall, however, there is often some added cost to cover the comparative dimension. After all, if the clients are requesting that one evaluate X because they are trying to decide between X and Y, there is really no way to avoid evaluating X against Y. Even if the clients do not mention Y, study of the context of the request for the evaluation will often uncover its existence as the phantom competitor.

There are some occasions when one can evaluate X against Y without running a full evaluation of X and of Y. One may be able to "shift the baseline" from zero to the Y level and just look for differences, a process that often involves little or no extra work compared to a straight evaluation of X. In evaluating sprinters, for example, we can run them against each other for about the same price as running one alone.

Frequently, it is necessary to add to these two alternatives, for example, because the evaluator sees another option that may offer more for less. The set of options among which the decision essentially lies, according to the evaluator's best judgment (and not necessarily according to the client's) is sometimes referred to as the set of "critical competitors." Experienced evaluators know that new-fangled approaches should always be run against tried—and formerly thought to be true—alternatives, and they know that innovators are often very nervous about those comparisons. The enthusiasts for the novel approach may jeer at the old style ("Everyone knows we've moved beyond *that*"), or they may argue that the comparison is unfair ("It's like comparing apples and oranges"), but the lesson of history is that allegedly mindless adherence to the supposedly medieval approach—in education, that is chalk and blackboard, paper and pencil, text and notepad, question and answer—is based on the extreme difficulty of doing any better for the kind of money that we are willing to spend.[15]

Similarly, the experienced evaluator knows that it is often worth running expensive programs against "el cheapo" alternatives, partly because the latter often turn out to be amazingly competitive and, in more than one well-known case, simply superior. And they have another advantage: Even if there is some loss in effectiveness, there may be a huge gain in market. Critical competitors will sometimes have to be invented, if they do not already exist. For example, an inexpensive alternative can often be constructed from a program that is pushing the cost ceiling by deliberately excluding the features that cost the most, if there is any chance at all that the program will still work. While program inventors are often inclined to think that no features can be removed without eliminating the payoff, experience shows that this is usually false, and the evaluators should make their own best judgments about how to define the critical competitors, usually with the help of specialist advice.

In the federal context, there is a special problem in identifying an appropriate set of critical competitors. The obvious competitors often include commercial products, and in the education field the political heat that arises from the private sector when an agency runs a horse race that shows the private sector entry to be inferior to the federally funded one, is generally viewed as unacceptable by agencies. On the other hand, not running the horse race leaves suspicions about whether the federal money was wasted. The contrast with the situation for the Food and Drug Administration or the Veterans Administration is depressing; in those fields, tough consumer-oriented evaluation is done without fear of political attack. Apparently, the job of getting the best education for children is not as important as getting the best drugs or hearing aids. It is possible that this situation is related to the ratio of the likelihood that congressional representatives will be going back to school to the likelihood that they will need medicine. We need to keep the pressure on government officials to change this situation in the federal field of education.

Missing Factor 6: Generalizability. One twist in serious evaluation that people tend to forget is an issue related to what Donald Campbell called "external validity." It is the issue of the larger significance of a program, project, or proposal. Can we generalize from the results of one evaluation to other important cases? For example, can we generalize from studies of new approaches to teaching some particular topic to conclusions about how to teach other topics, perhaps even to other subjects, to other grades, other student populations, other teachers, other schools and areas, other countries, other times, other versions? Answers to these questions depend on knowledge of the relevant variables governing education effectiveness, and on judgments about the kind of sample used in the study under immediate consideration, both of which are risky business. But we should attempt to answer the question of generalizability simply because of the vast difference in the value of a program that can be treated as a pilot—as a first step toward major improvements across a broad spectrum—in comparison to a stand-alone effort whose merits depend entirely on the benefits to those affected during the lifetime of the program. This issue brings up, among other matters, the issue of marketability or exportability of the program. It should also lead to consideration of modifications that would affect generalizability in relation to other versions and to other markets.

The reference to generalization to other times has more buried in it than may be obvious at first sight. The reference is not only to repeatability at the same site—a nontrivial matter because of the loss of novelty effects, changes in personnel, fatigue, and gains in experience—but also to the durability of the program across time. The feature of generalizability commonly runs into trouble because the infrastructure fails, for example, the company supplying the software goes out of business or the guru who did the program's troubleshooting goes into retirement. The question of generalizability thus forces the evaluator to look at a program from a broader perspective than found in the site-focused, particularistic approach that was at one stage dominant in program evaluation and is still close to the heart of the rich description, negotiation, and other particularistic approaches. In certain respects, this consideration provides a key connection with research, because it not only draws on research in order to reach conclusions but also can contribute to research if new evidence is found to support the conclusions.

Missing Factor 7: Synthesis. If a program has one goal, specified in measurable terms, then the process of checking to see if it has been achieved yields a simple yes or no answer. We call this measurement rather than evaluation. In the real world, things are more complex in four ways, and these complexities introduce the need for another skill in the evaluator. First, the number of goals becomes larger; second, many of them are not specified in behavioral terms; third, the goals have different relative importance; fourth, the program's achievements involve dimensions that were not part of the goals. So the results make up a complex pattern of success and failure on the various dimensions. The upshot is that the empirical part of the investigation leaves the evaluator with a mass of data that must be integrated in order to get, or to discover that one cannot get, an overall conclusion, whether it is a ranking or a rating. How does one achieve data integration? The tradition has been to say that "this is where judgment comes in," which of course raises the question of whether the judgment is entirely arbitrary or can be judged as good or bad. And if the latter, the further question is, obviously, What standards apply to this integrative step? The values-free doctrinaires of course favor the view that there are no such standards and that the judgment is essentially arbitrary; and the evaluation texts do not offer an objective alternative. If evaluation is to achieve the status of a discipline, some kind of reasonably objective procedure must be provided for this step. So far, this procedure has rarely been included in the job description or the training of evaluators (see Thesis 19).

Summary. To sum up the general implications of Thesis 1, we must move evaluation away from the task of determining a program's progress toward its goals and instead emphasize the task of determining its comparative cost-effectiveness in meeting needs, integrating into this conclusion consideration of unexpected outcomes, generalizability, and various value standards, including those from needs assessments, ethics, the law, and other relevant disciplines. Does this mean that a contract let for investigative goal achievement determination should not be called an evaluation contract? Well, one can call it a goal achievement evaluation, if that makes anyone feel better. It is better to design the contract so that it will yield both monitoring information and serious reporting on the other matters, specified above, that go into determining the merit or worth of a program. This is still goal-based evaluation, but conscientious goal-based evaluation can do a very good job. It is, however, better still to design the evaluation so that it involves a goal-free component, in which the evaluators are isolated from the goals, and the staff of the program and formative evaluation.

Thesis 2: Program evaluation is not applied social science

This thesis is a corollary of Thesis 1. The brevity with which it is formulated in the heading is a little uncompromising. There is an interesting although radical way of retaining program evaluation within the social sciences: by redefining the social sciences. So a kinder and gentler, but excessively discursive, heading would be as follows: "Program evaluation is not applied social science as that discipline has been thought of by its practitioners until now, but it may be the discipline that leads social science to expand its previously narrow self-concept." Here, however, I address the view that program evaluation should not be regarded as part of social science, as currently conceived. That is the view incorporated into the definition of program evaluation in Rossi and Freeman (1989).

Arguments for Exclusion. First, the main reason for the negative position expressed in Thesis 2 is, of course, the essential involvement of direct (unconditional) value claims in the conclusions of program evaluations (for example, "This approach is one of the best available for teaching the elements of computer-assisted design to first-year engineering students"), an anathema to most social scientists. If they were to give in on this, then program evaluation could be said to be part of (a better-conceived) social science. But their unwillingness to draw unconditional evaluative conclusions precludes them from doing useful evaluation.[16]

The commonsense view, in contrast, must surely be that since it is possible to conclude, on the basis of good evidence, that a particular can opener is overpriced and ineffective, then it is possible to draw the same kind of conclusion from evidence about a particular computerized elementary school science package. It seems reasonable to suppose that social scientists are able to answer that kind of question, just as medical scientists can answer an analogous question about a diet or drug regimen.

Second, problems about the ethics of program practices are as crucial a part of program evaluation as any other, and certainly ethics is one area where the social scientists' training usually leaves them completely unprepared, and unwilling, to contribute. There are corresponding cases in product evaluation such as the use of ozone killers in air conditioners, but the negative judgment is more easily separable from the basic process of evaluation there than in the case of, say, social studies programs that lack thorough discussions of Southerners' arguments for slavery in the era of the American Civil War.

Third, in considering whether to include program evaluation in the social sciences, there are also serious questions about other matters such as whether one should treat cost analysis as part of social science. Certainly, it is not part of the standard training for social scientists except for the few that happen into the subset of program evaluation courses that address it, and it hardly seems part of the usual conception of social science.

Finally, other missing elements in social science self-concept and training, and hence weaknesses in the view that program evaluation is applied social science, include (1) skill in judging specialized content quality, which the subspecialty of curriculum evaluation is well developed to incorporate without resigning in favor of the use of content experts; (2) skill in judging the extent to which the program meets relevant legal standards; (3) the same with respect to accounting standards; (4) the extra presentational and audience needs assessment skills involved in producing good evaluation reports by contrast with research reports; (5) skills in product evaluation, which are frequently required, as in the evaluation of supplies, communications systems (local area networks, pagers, and so on), computers and computer programs, and administrative support equipment; (6) teaching skills, or as Cronbach and others (1980, Thesis 93) put it, only a little too strongly, "The evaluator is an educator; his success is to be judged by what others learn"; and (7) money management, as in the difference between compliance and smart investment or management of working capital and prepayment monies, and as in smart purchasing policies for supplies and equipment.

It is a charitable judgment that keeps one from listing another reason, the weakness of almost all social science training in the area of personnel evaluation.[17] That has become a specialty in which the few specialist social scientists who know something about it match mastery with the lawyers, but it has hardly become part of the standard training of social scientists. Another candidate for a discipline often essential in the practice of evaluation that dwells far outside the realm of social science is logic, since the key to validating evaluations lies in that domain, not within the social sciences. However, it is not formal logic that helps here, and legal training may be just as good for detecting the key slips in the inference chains that are used to justify evaluative conclusions.

Of course, no one person is going to embody true expertise in all of the fields listed above, although a good evaluator should try to acquire at least a minimum competence in each. (For example, one can reasonably argue that it is not the job of the program evaluator to decide whether the program office exhibits massive waste of resources through the purchase of overpriced or unreliable equipment. However, while not part of the core body of skills of a program evaluator, the ability to pick up these clues to bad management is surely better than the inability to do so.) The point of the long list is to make clear that program evaluation is not properly regarded as part of applied social science in anything like the usual sense of the latter term. It is an activity typically requiring a unique assembly of skills, and while some of the important ones come from social science, many others come from outside it. This is why a team, or an evaluator using several consultants, is so often the appropriate approach.

Summary. The commonsensical view of the situation is to think that even the most frequently needed skills in program evaluation include substantial expertise in a number of disciplines besides the social sciences, and that particular program evaluations often require very extensive, additional expertise. This line of argument is perfectly compatible with the view that social science training is useful for program evaluators, and that some individuals with social science training are good evaluators by virtue of having learned many extra skills and having unlearned old attitudes. However, there are no grounds to think that, on balance, social science training, by itself, equips them better than the training of a lawyer, an accountant, a logician, or a professional manager, all of whom will also need substantial further training and collaborators.

Arguments for Inclusion, with Rebuttals. First, the main basis for the idea that program evaluation is applied social science is, presumably, that social science training does provide the repertoire of survey and testing skills that are very important in large-scale evaluations. But that very training carries with it the biases of an establishment position. The sloppy thinking about statistical significance (see Thesis 18) and the synthesis process (see Thesis 19) was presumably due to the fact that the social science culture indoctrinated novices into these fallacies as part of the "accepted practice" package, and that indoctrination was made more acceptable by the exclusion of tough evaluation from the social science disciplines. Current beliefs about the desirability or dispensability of fully controlled studies for research purposes in the social sciences are likely to be given too much weight in decisions on the best design for a program evaluation study, where the issue needs to be dealt with on evaluation-specific as well as case-specific grounds.[18] The same problem at a more general level arises with respect to what Robert Stake refers to as "pre-ordinate" designs for evaluation. Very often in evaluation, one turns up responses in the early phases of a survey, for example, that should lead to a major redefinition of the sample and the survey instrument (for example, when a respondent volunteers information about illegal procedures [sexual harassment] or when there are unanticipated beneficial side effects in the free-response invitation at the end of the interview). This situation comes hard to those who are highly trained in normal survey techniques, especially if they have set up a proposal or an RFP (request for proposal) for an evaluation that allocated a certain sum to a well-defined survey.

There are still many examples of superficial assumptions that have been enshrined for fifty years in the test and measurement literature, one part of the social sciences. One example is the treatment of affective measures, which still suffers from confusion about the relation of attitudes to beliefs.[19] Another is the use of test results and other indicators for personnel evaluation on the basis of "empirical validation," that is, mere correlations with the criterion variables, although in most cases their use on this basis is scientifically as well as ethically (and often legally) illicit (see Thesis 18). Perhaps the worst is the naive belief that multiple-choice tests are the most general objective (that is, machine-scorable) type of tests. This fallacy is reiterated in Thorndike, 1990. The point is that there are equally objective (machine-scorable) tests that avoid essentially all of the objections to multiple-choice tests; they are described as multiple-rating tests and discussed in Scriven, 1991. These are the kinds of fundamental errors that the logician or lawyer often spots much faster than someone brought up to accept them as part of the received doctrine. On occasion, of course, social scientists have recognized these errors, as in the early skirmishes about the scientific significance of significance tests and the concept of test validity, where measurement theorists are only now beginning to sort it out, very late in the history of its use.

A second fallacious reason for thinking that evaluation is part of social science involves the belief that the task of evaluation is to understand or explain the social phenomena involved in a program. Evaluation has as little concern with understanding and explaining as measurement does. The task of evaluation is essentially the determination of merit, worth, or value, and it is a hard enough task without tossing in the kind of obligation that the social sciences have rightly regarded as part of their mandate but have never been very successful at fulfilling. Here is Cronbach and others' (1980) Thesis 15: "Evaluation is better used to understand events and processes for the sake of guiding future activities." That is a very appropriate task for applied social science, but it would be suicidal for evaluation to shoulder it. Even Cronbach and others' Thesis 1 seems inflated in its sense of the mission of evaluation: "Program evaluation is a process whereby society learns about itself." In a small way, perhaps; true to about the same degree that product evaluation is a process whereby technology learns about itself. Mostly, however, program and product evaluations are just processes whereby consumers learn one kind of thing about programs and products: their merit or worth and perhaps the dimensions of that merit and worth. That is a rather small slice of "society learning about itself." It is better to tie evaluation to practical progress rather than to intellectual or scientific understanding; we can make little progress with anything from social planning to drug design if we cannot do good evaluations.

Third, a related reason that is often implicit if not explicit in the argument for treating program evaluation as part of social science is that the task of evaluation requires the evaluator to understand the working of programs in order to evaluate them, and programs are, after all, social phenomena. This view is incorporated in the theory-driven model (see Chen, 1990) of program evaluation, a recent addition to the list of models. In any significant sense of "theory," this view is clearly false since "black-box" evaluations, in which the evaluator knows nothing about the machinery inside the box, can often yield the key conclusions. The situation is not too different from that in the evaluation of complex artifacts by those who know nothing about the engineering that is required to build them. Road testers who know something about automobile engineering can contribute something useful on occasion, but that knowledge is not essential and it often introduces bias (technicism, or the substitution of specifications for performance). In the social arena, the highly dubious nature of most theories of social phenomena make it much less likely that we can improve our program evaluations by appeal to social theory, and quite likely that we shall weaken them.

It is true that an evaluation will often benefit from the advice, preferably, the participation, of someone with local expertise, that is, knowledge of the workings of the kind of program being evaluated. However, one very rarely needs anything that qualifies as a theory of the phenomena occurring in the program, by contrast with working experience of similar programs. Certainly, evaluations involving only folk psychology, experience, and careful observation of process often do very well. Perhaps knowledge of theory can best be seen as a source of possible directions for investigation by the evaluator.

A fourth, somewhat different reason for the view under consideration is that the practice of evaluation is correctly recognized as a highly complex social phenomenon, the study of which certainly falls under the purview of the social sciences. This view is apparent in many of Cronbach and others' (1980) ninety-five theses. For example, their Thesis 11 says, "A theory of evaluation must be as much a theory of political interaction as it is a theory of how to determine facts" (p. 3). This view confounds two perfectly proper studies: (1) the descriptive theory of evaluation as a political (psychological, economic, and so on) phenomenon and (2) the prescriptive theory of evaluation, that is, the logic and methodology of the discipline. Evaluation is certainly a proper subject for descriptive analysis by the social sciences, as are, for example, the politics and prejudices of the social sciences establishment. A descriptive theory of the phenomenon of program evaluation will involve a description of how it operates in practice, an explanation of its social effects and of associated political phenomena, and, perhaps, even predictions about how it will work in certain political contexts. This is just like a descriptive theory of the political phenomena surrounding the legitimation and use of the abortifacient RU486, the morning-after pill.

A prescriptive theory of evaluation is not concerned with explaining the political process at all, although it will have to include some parameters such as the probable credibility of different approaches to the audiences involved, which are affected by political considerations. A prescriptive theory of evaluation, like a prescriptive theory of measurement, defines the basic concepts, establishes their interrelationship, and derives conclusions from them about how to solve typical problems in evaluation, that is, prescriptions. Since evaluation works in a political context (speaking loosely), like everything else, some of the solutions will involve reference to what to do in certain political contexts. But it is not part of the job of a prescriptive theory of evaluation to explain—certainly not to develop theories about—the political phenomena associated with evaluation, any more than it is part of a prescriptive theory about RU486 to provide theories about political opposition to and support for it. A prescriptive theory about RU486 is an account of how and why it is supposed to work and how it should be used, that is, prescribed.

Now, there is a type of practical wisdom that deals with the use of evaluation (or birth control) in a particular political context. This wisdom can be picked up from experienced "old hands," like most political savvy, but it is notorious for the conflicting opinions encountered among equally experienced pundits. To describe this kind of knowledge as a theory is exaggerated, and to call it a part of evaluation theory (or, in the analogy, birth control theory) is doubly unwarranted. True, economics has taken the same kind of contradictory advice and made multiple theories out of it, accompanied by the smoke and mirrors of mathematics, but the failure of the results to meet the minimum standards of validity for scientific theories makes it an example that one should try to avoid rather than emulate.

The risk of Cronbach and others' (1980) approach is that it dilutes attention to the crucial core theory of evaluation by suggesting that "a theory of political interaction" should play a major role in it. While any general account of evaluation should make some reference to descriptive "theories"—really, just observations and speculations—about the phenomenon of evaluation, it is entirely improper to suggest that evaluation theory should involve any reference to political interaction, for that is not an evaluative concept. One might as well argue that a theory of fundamental particles in physics should involve a theory of political interaction because politics is an essential part of the process of funding the accelerators and supercolliders where most of the research proceeds.

Summary. Evaluation is an extraordinarily demanding discipline, and practice in even one subarea such as program evaluation requires some understanding of a broad range of subject matter and some ability within a broad repertoire of skills. It is therefore nearly always best done as a collaborative effort. Now, there are significantly different ways of running such collaborations. We are all used to having subject matter consultants to call on, but the idea of the subject matter as a kind of expertise that one plugs into an evaluation design is ill-conceived. Too often it leads us to overlook absolutely fundamental points in the presuppositions and overall picture (see Thesis 17).[20]

A commonly useful procedure for education program evaluation is to use a team of three, all of them with at least some training or experience in evaluation. There is no need to think that this is an expensive approach; the work is shared and should only take at most one-third as long for each person, in comparison to these three each doing or running a program evaluation of their own. One member of the team should have a strong subject matter background and should call in further specialist help where necessary; another member should be quantitatively strong; and the third should be strong on the qualitative and non–social science aspects of evaluation. Only the second of these is likely to be a social science major, in the ideal team; and even then, he or she should be a born-again social scientist, that is, one who has come to see the legitimacy and utility of direct evaluative conclusions.

Thesis 3: Program evaluation is neither a dominant nor an autonomous field of evaluation

This thesis is intended to place program evaluation in perspective within the discipline of evaluation, just as Thesis 2 is intended to place it in perspective among other disciplines. Thesis 3 is best tackled in two stages. First, I set out the array of pieces on the evaluation board. Second, I look at the connections among them.

Program Evaluation Is Only One of Many Fields of Applied Evaluation. The applied areas in evaluation include the Big Six: product evaluation, performance evaluation, personnel evaluation, program evaluation, proposal evaluation, and policy evaluation. Each of these has a substantial history, many current practitioners linked by professional organizations (sometimes several), and a place in at least some current graduate training programs. There are two other applied fields deserving special attention. The first is the evaluation of evaluations (meta-evaluation), which is a key field because of its control role. The second is a field comprising a set of fields: It might be called "intradisciplinary evaluation," the evaluation of the data, sources, explanations, definitions, classifications, theories, designs, predictions, contributors, journals, and so on within the discipline. This evaluation process goes on as part of the life of the disciplines, since there are the entities that make up the process and products of a discipline. In toto, intradisciplinary evaluation is by far the largest part of evaluation, and having practitioners do it with reasonable skill is the price of admission to the company of disciplines. Other applied fields besides the Big Six range from literary criticism and real estate appraisal to quality control in industry.

In a historical perspective, there are thousands of years of personnel and performance evaluation behind us, the Chinese civil service examinations and the first Olympic games being quite late entries.[21] Systematic product evaluation began tens of thousands of years earlier. One subfield of it had reached the status of a hereditary profession by the great age of the medieval Japanese swordsmiths. So program evaluation in any systematic sense is not a very large part or a very ancient part of evaluation.

My earlier remarks about the need to go beyond the social sciences for program evaluation expertise indicate one dimension in which we need to broaden our perspective on program evaluation. But we need to broaden it much further to include several of the other applied fields within evaluation. While Rossi and Freeman's (1989) book is titled *Evaluation: A Systematic Approach,* they in fact have covered only a fragment of evaluation. Their book title reflects the geocentric attitude found in other areas of applied evaluation—the view that the area of evaluation in which the author works is all there is to evaluation. This insularity was perhaps a way to avoid confrontation with the politically correct idea that no *general* field of evaluation was legitimate. The narrowness was often even more extreme. For example, books in the fields of education and psychology published during the first fifty or sixty years of this century often had the unqualified word or words *evaluation* or *educational evaluation* in their titles.[22] All that these terms referred to was the testing of students (occasionally, in psychology, the reference was to the testing of other subjects, such as applicants for jobs). The idea that in education, for example, one might use the word evaluation to refer to the evaluation of teachers, curricula, administrators, programs, or schools was simply unrecognized. Nor were these omissions mentioned and explained in the introductions of the books; the writers simply thought that, or at least wrote as if, their books encompassed the universe of educational evaluation.

Presumably, those who acted as if program evaluation was the only legitimate field would not, if asked, deny the existence of product evaluation or personnel evaluation. Perhaps they never thought of these other fields as on an intellectual par with program evaluation; otherwise, some explanation for using the common titles and ignoring the hard-won lessons from the other areas would have been appropriate.

There was another latent function of these restrictive views of evaluation. They served to reinforce the power of management. Evaluation of personnel and programs was one of the traditional and defensible functions of powerholders. It seemed natural to them that evaluation meant that kind of evaluation. The idea that evaluation meant more than this—that the barons should also be evaluated, and in a way that would involve the peasants' input, was (dimly) perceived as undermining their power.

It is easy to understand why administrators were more enthusiastic about evaluating underlings than evaluating themselves. Nobody really likes going to the dentist, even for regular checkups that do not hurt, because there is always the possibility of receiving bad news, with its consequent pain and cost. However, the very argument used by managers to justify personnel and program evaluation in the face of opposition—effectiveness maximization—applies considerably more strongly to the evaluation of managers, given the greater relative leverage on effectiveness that supervisors have in comparison with supervisees. In the education system, the student was the powerless party, at least until the rebellions of the 1960s at the college level, so evaluation in education was naturally thought of as the evaluation of students.

In psychology and psychiatry, the powerless were the subjects, candidates, or patients; recent work on their rights has done a good deal to change the exploitation that accompanied this powerlessness, but less to ensure adequate evaluation of the professionals. In books on psychological evaluation, the notions of proper test administration and test validity were considered extensively. These constitute a part of test evaluation (along with an examination of cost, side effects, competitors, and so on) and hence a part of a broader concept of evaluation. A modest broadening would have included the use of tests to evaluate the quality of work by the psychologist. But in fact tests were seen to have just one function: evaluation of subordinate others, not oneself, one's own work, or one's peers' work.

A major factor in this widespread tendency to take a very narrow view of evaluation was probably the ideological taboo on evaluation as a legitimate full-citizenship discipline. Since it was obvious to the practitioners in each area that some kind of practical evaluation was not only possible but also a task that required special knowledge and skills if it was to be done well, they just went ahead with their local efforts to develop the subject within a severely circumscribed area. Had they flown any higher—

had they started looking at the general nature of evaluation in their discipline or across the board—they would have been shot down by the values police patrolling the metatheoretical skies. The result of this restriction in each applied field of evaluation was a near-fatal failure to recognize, let alone learn from and contribute to, other, often well-developed fields of evaluation.

What was lacking was an overview. There were a number of interesting attempts to provide this within a particular field of evaluation. The most fertile field was education program evaluation, where a dozen models appeared and were christened, and still have their supporters today. But these models only refer to a very limited part of evaluation and reflect that insularity in more than subject matter. It is essential to realize that evaluation is an overarching discipline, one that not only has a dozen well-developed applied areas but also has a core discipline that only now is beginning to be recognized as such.

There is a close analogy between evaluation and a subject such as statistics, which has not only distinctive areas of application associated with biology, demography, psychology, quantum mechanics, and so on but also a core mathematical discipline. The difference from evaluation is that statistics had access to an existing core in probability theory as its applied fields developed, whereas in evaluation the very idea of such a core subject was dismissed (or relegated to philosophy, in which little was done with it), so the applied areas developed on their own. A closer analogy is perhaps with measurement, where the practices developed extensively before the theory of scaling emerged.

Program Evaluation Is Not a Stand-Alone Field of Evaluation. In the transdisciplinary view, the applied areas in evaluation are logically and methodologically dependent on a core theory of evaluation, not just a theory of *program* evaluation. An explicit version of this core theory did not exist until very recently, and the feeble implicit versions were seriously invalid in several ways. Moreover, the applied areas overlap with each other in complex ways, and the lack of an overview—something provided by a core account—got us into trouble because we were very slow to see the overlaps. For example, program evaluation, as it has been conventionally conceived in the literature, involves no reference to personnel evaluation, as one can see by checking the indexes of the texts and anthologies. Yet, our common sense tells us that good program evaluation often uncovers and correctly reports on poor management or great creative talent in some aspect of the program (Paul Rosenbloom of Minnemath comes to mind as an example of the latter).

These evaluative references to personnel, which often amount to subevaluations within the total program evaluation, are there for the commonsense reason that programs cannot run without personnel and indeed are highly dependent on the personnel for their success. Surely, then, one should treat personnel evaluation as a significant element in program evaluation. So where is the relevant expertise being taught to program evaluators? It is not in the texts, and it is not in any training programs of which I am aware. Instead, it is way over there in industrial and organizational psychology or education administration courses (for education programs) or in schools of business. Personnel evaluation is a substantial area that has accumulated surprising results, and these can significantly affect the evaluation of programs, as can be seen by browsing the literature (for example, the essay titled "Personnel Evaluation" in Rosenzweig and Porter, 1991). Education has led the way here in developing *The Personnel Evaluation Standards* (Joint Committee on Standards for Educational Evaluation Staff, 1988). The neglect of personnel evaluation in the middle period of evaluation's new era is a match for the story of complete neglect of cost analysis in the early years of program evaluation.

A similar argument can be used to show that program evaluation often cannot avoid involvement in product evaluation, for example, the evaluation of laboratory equipment or computer software for an education program in writing or engineering. And it often cannot avoid proposal evaluation, for example, the evaluation of the National Science Foundation program in the Physics Division, where a great deal of the effort relates to funding research via a proposals process. It is not surprising that texts in program evaluation do not mention these other branches of evaluation, although they are often relevant to program evaluations, and in a way that is quite different from the way in which subject matter disciplines come into the evaluation of education programs, because there is no well-defined pool of general practice experts to whom one can turn for consulting help on such matters, unlike the situation in personnel evaluation.[23]

All of this discussion of the dependence of program evaluation on other parts of evaluation, however, is dominated by the dependence on the logic of evaluation, part of what I have called the core discipline of evaluation. What is in the core discipline of evaluation, if we allow that the subject has been liberated to the point where its practitioners can be permitted a self-concept? The map of the applied areas is there, with commentary on the overlap and inconsistencies among them; so too are the whole logic of evaluation, which includes such topics as multi-attribute utility methodology and the way in which evaluative conclusions can legitimately be inferred from factual and definitional premises; the taxonomy of evaluative predicates and the different methodologies required to establish conclusions containing them; the dimensions of evaluations; the models of evaluation; the relation of evaluation to other disciplines; and so on.

So there *is* a broad view of evaluation, and program evaluation has a place within that view. We might also note that the broad view is also a grand view. Evaluation, the ugly frog, turns into a prince when the spell on us is broken. Evaluation is all that distinguishes astronomy from astrology, good explanations from bad ones, good experimental designs—or bridge designs—from inferior ones, good scientists and engineers and technologists from run-of-the-mill ones. It is a discipline that is part of every discipline because it distinguishes a discipline from pretentious jargon, just as it distinguishes good food from garbage.

The idea that science should be values-free is simply a contradiction in terms, since what science should be is an evaluative decision, and it is hard to argue that there is a more important kind of decision anywhere in science. This is the decision, or a refinement of it, after all, that we call on many of our peer review panels to make. In particular, we ask them to review the scientific *quality* of the proposals in front of them. They are indeed evaluators, and on them and on their peers on editorial boards and appointment committees rests the whole definition and quality of science, and eventually the whole future of science—and of mathematics, and engineering, and technology. To suggest that what they do is improper is to stand this issue on its head; it is the suggestion that is improper, the suggestion that quality control has no place in science. If it does, then science is at its core as well as in all of its applications an evaluative enterprise.

If science is an evaluative enterprise, then where in the whole of science and scientific training is the training in evaluation? It is not there. Like grammar, evaluation, to the extent allowable and in the forms allowed, is supposed to be inhaled from the atmosphere in which the scientist grows up. This is an excellent arrangement if the quality of the content of texts allegedly reporting the current state of knowledge is all that is to be evaluated. If, on the other hand, proposals for the development of new paradigms and for nonstandard research, general procedures for evaluating research, the worth of pure research, applicants for a job in a science department, and the quality of scientific education are to be evaluated, along with a dozen other things that do not fall within the standard field in which the scientist is trained, then the evidence is overwhelmingly against success, as many of the thirty-one theses in this volume attest. Scientists are not known for their outstanding skills in stock market or real estate investment, not even for their success when moving from distinguished careers in the physical sciences into mathematics, let alone into the social sciences. This is just because good skills in scientific method in one field do not transfer into good analytical skills in other specialized fields—and evaluation is one such field. Thinking skills are strongly localized, and to the extent to which they can be generalized, the route to success is to make these skills explicit. When evaluation was seen as a nondiscipline, this task was impossible.

The set of theses listed here addresses the consequences of the
transdisciplinary view for popular views of program evaluation.

Implications for Popular Evaluation Approaches

This is a short chapter because the argument for most of the theses here is presented in Chapter One, in the discussion about the limitations of monitoring and extended monitoring, or goal achievement evaluation. Based on my recent work in upgrading a design for a large state program (Public Law 620b in California) into a full-scale evaluation, I can verify that there is nothing trivial about large monitoring programs, let alone goal achievement evaluation, anymore now than in the 1960s when the new era in program evaluation began. For better or for worse, monitoring and goal achievement evaluation can miss many aspects of a program that need improvement and leave the evaluator open to a dozen flaws in the reasoning behind recommendations to continue, terminate, curtail, or supplement a program. The next thesis simply points to one of those loopholes; others are picked up later.

Thesis 4: Side effects are often the main point

Side effects were a latent killer for a literal interpretation of goal achievement evaluation. They cannot be ignored because they may require the abandonment of an otherwise successful program or the salvation of an otherwise unsuccessful program. But it is hard to design an investigation to find them, since they are, more or less by definition, unanticipated. How do we design an evaluation that will detect side effects? The only systematic methodology for detecting side effects is the goal-free approach, one of several reasons for using it. It is not particularly expensive: Only one person is needed on it, or just a consultant, and only for part of the life of the evaluation. Individuals try it and are surprised by what turns up. They then need only evaluate the side effects found against all relevant values and they have graduated from monitoring school.

Thesis 5: Subject matter expertise may be the right hand of education program and proposal evaluation, but one cannot wrap things up with a single hand

The federal agencies, egged on by the professions, are great advocates of the peer review process, and peer review does provide an essential element in evaluation. But the evaluation of programs—and, by analogy, many proposals—requires one to judge more than content, as we have seen; and skills in judging these other matters are not usually or systematically taken into account when panelists are selected. Even with proposal evaluation, the main task is predictive rather than content-evaluative; and one cannot predict success from the quality of content, one can only predict failure from the absence of that quality. In most cases, proposals come from people with reasonable or high competence in the subject matter area, so the principal expertise of the usual panel has little relevance once it has been used to ensure the price of admission. The panel lacks training in the skills that are relevant, notably, the skills of looking past the halo of high research ability to evaluate the soundness of management plans, the past track record in project completion, the cost analyses, the critical competitors in science, mathematics, engineering, and technology (SMET) education, the needs assessment, the generalizability, and the many other matters that come into proposal evaluation. When we start talking about proposals in the area of SMET education, several other domains of knowledge become relevant, and subject matter expertise takes up a still smaller part of the necessary skills.

Of course, most of us think that we can evaluate programs, and so we serve on panels to do it from a sense of duty, or a lust for power. But most of us are just amateurs at it, as any competent evaluator serving on (or serving as program officer for) the panels soon sees. As one might expect, the interpanel reliability is poor.[24] Of course, this is a hot political issue since Big Science, in particular, wants to own the turf and so does not want its limited competence in managing its own affairs revealed. This is an expensive self-indulgence at a time when our place in world-class SMET needs all the help that it can get.

Serious efforts to improve the situation might go as follows. First, the Band-Aid: We construct some simple calibration materials (hypothetical applications) and train the panelists for two hours (they need more, but they might put up with that much) to spot the main traps into which they regularly fall (halo effect, "mythical man-month," paradigm protection, bullying, and so on).

Second, the long-term solution: We set up a data base of panelists and their ratings, feed back into it the ratings of later judgments of success and failure of projects (funded and unfunded) made by peers (this is what they are good at), and run the correlations between ratings and success of the projects on which there is high agreement about success and failure. The estimates of success should be corrected at, say, three-year intervals, and subject to review by the best people in the field. This procedure will certainly uncover a baseline hit rate, useful for reality orientation, and ideally will flag those panelists who are outstanding evaluators as well as those who randomly hit and miss. We should then weight the ratings of panelists according to their past success, perhaps on a .5 to 2.0 scale (known weak to known excellent); use the winners more frequently; drop those below 1.0 after an N of, say, 30; use the winners as leaders and trainers, if they agree to serve and show signs of having these extra skills; and start work on finding out how to match their skills with an expert system. Consideration should be given to paying raters by results in order to get their attention and to get the nonplayers back into the pool. The investment would pay for itself many times over.

Third, it would not hurt to have a data base of principal investigators, de jure and de facto, and to get a track record on them (although the rater data base is more important). It would be ideal if we could identify in the data base the reasons why projects that failed did fail. For example, was it because of incompetent cost analysis leading to an unmarketable product, or because the project could not be completed within the planned budget? With this type of information, we could find out where we need to improve the panelist training program.

Fourth, we need to find and try out solutions for the other great weakness of the panels—the conservative bias on which most critics seem to agree. There are promising fixes for this problem, and they need to be tested properly (see Thesis 28).

Thesis 6: Evaluation designs without provision for evaluation of the evaluation are unclear on the concept

Evaluation, like psychology, is a reflexive discipline: It applies to itself and to its practitioners. One might say, "Evaluation begins at home." An evaluator who does not have a well thought out answer to the question "Who evaluates the evaluator?" has not done much thinking about evaluation. Some evaluators, asked that question by a client, say, "Why, you do." That is the beginning of an answer, but it is incomplete because it is like a doctor saying that the patient should be the judge of the quality of the doctor's advice. The patient is in a position to judge only some aspects of the advice, such as its comprehensibility, relevance, and quality in terms of end result. The technical part of the advice requires evaluation by someone who is competent at the technicalities, hence, in the medical case, the notion of "a second opinion." That is what we need in the case of substantial evaluations, and it helps credibility—and often validity—to get the advice from someone whom the client picks, if that is feasible. The evaluator might offer the client several choices and encourage him or her to find others. For a big program, this meta-evaluation should be done in the first place as formative evaluation to improve the design, perhaps again to improve the implementation, and then, summatively, on the final report to provide perspective in interpretation. A maximum of one day of consulting for each of these functions is needed, unless real trouble shows up, even for a big program. Since the consultation can often be done quite well from the documents and through telephone calls, without travel expenses, the cost is considerably less than the cost of mistakes due to faulty evaluation design or conclusions.

A good evaluator should include arrangements for the meta-evaluation in the design of an evaluation because he or she should expect to get benefits for the design and implementation of the evaluation being evaluated, just as others get benefits from being evaluated. Moreover, the evaluator knows that the client will benefit from the increased credibility provided by an independent meta-evaluator's report.

Although the evaluator should make provisions for a meta-evaluator, the evaluator should not pick the summative meta-evaluator because of the loss of credibility in that arrangement. The evaluator may, however, pick a formative meta-evaluator on the basis of known excellence and ability to communicate.

It is always worth considering parallel evaluations since they sometimes serve the purpose of meta-evaluation better than a meta-evaluation. Often, given budget limitations for evaluation, it is much better to spend money on two concurrent evaluations—by teams that are forbidden to communicate with each other—than it is on one large evaluation, even if the parallel evaluations are underbudgeted by common standards. The evidence suggests that interjudge agreement on evaluative conclusions is extremely variable. So unless there are strong reasons for thinking that the case in point is routine or that the funds would not allow anything worthwhile from the two half-price investigations, the double evaluation will be more valuable to the client than will a mere second opinion. In particular, the double evaluation avoids the substantial possibility of bias due to the fact that the meta-evaluator knows what the first evaluator has concluded (see Thesis 27), and it produces an excellent climate of putting both teams on their mettle. There are, of course, many people who do not like that climate. They should not be given evaluation contracts unless they can propose a better way to get a result of known reliability.

So, in answer to the question of who evaluates the evaluator, the evaluator should arrange for at least one approach and expect the client to comment on its suitability; the evaluator can offer a range of further options, though the use of at least one other is strongly recommended. Eventually, clients will be sophisticated enough—and educated enough by good evaluators—to build some of these options into the design.

Thesis 7: An evaluation without a recommendation is like a fish without a bicycle

It is widely thought that program evaluations should always conclude with a recommendations section, but this view is based on a misunderstanding of the logic of evaluation, and the misunderstanding has seriously unfortunate effects.[25] The conclusion of an evaluation is normally a statement or set of statements about the merit, worth, or value of something, probably with several qualifications (for example, "These materials on planetary astronomy are probably the best available, for middle-school students with well-developed vocabularies"). There is a considerable step from the conclusion to the recommendations (for example, "You should buy these materials for this school"), and it is a step that evaluators are often not well qualified to make. For example, in teacher evaluation, an evaluator, or, for that matter, a student, may be able to identify a bad teacher conclusively. But it does not follow that the teacher should be fired or remediated or even told about the result of the evaluation (which may be informal). In making one of those recommendations, the evaluator must have highly specific local knowledge (for example, about the terms of the teacher's contract, the possibility of early retirement, and temporary traumas in the teacher's home life) and special expertise (for example, about the legal situation), both of which go a long way beyond the skills necessary for evaluation. If the evaluator is looking at recommendations aimed not at actions but at improvement (for example, suggested changes in the way in which the teacher organizes the lesson and changes in the frequency of question-asking), then he or she moves into an area requiring still further dimensions of expertise.

Now, people often say, and many evaluators agree, that evaluation aimed at mere judgments (summative evaluation) is not worth much, or certainly not worth as much as evaluation aimed at improvement (formative evaluation). They take this to mean that an evaluation should provide not just recommendations for action but recommendations for improvement. This is a gross misconception, possible only because we have paid little attention to the logical geography of distinctions among evaluation, recommendations, and remediation. Certainly, from the manager's point of view in program evaluation, it is an attractive proposition to get suggestions for improvement; from the evaluee's point of view in personnel evaluation, it is a plus to get suggestions for improvement; but from the (third-party) consumer's point of view, in any kind of evaluation, such suggestions are absurd.

To suppose the contrary is an example of the cost of failing to look across the barriers separating applied fields in evaluation. Let us look at the situation in product evaluation. What the consumer wants from a product evaluation (and also from a program evaluation, and also from teacher evaluation) is summative evaluation, as clear and as simple as is possible to make it. That is, the consumer wants to know which products are best and which are inferior, unsatisfactory, shoddy, or unsafe. If there is something that the consumer would like to have in addition to the bare summative ratings, it is not a set of instructions on which products to buy (a matter for the consumer to work out with respect to his or her own budget and family priorities) and not a set of suggestions about how the products might be improved. Rather, of interest are details about the differential strengths and weaknesses of the products. The species of summative evaluation that provides those details is called analytical summative—by comparison with global summative—and it typically costs more to get but is more useful for matching the results to personal preferences.

In program evaluation, what the taxpayer and potential user want to know are the cost and the effectiveness of the available programs. So they would prefer to get an analytical summative evaluation, if they can afford it, since it will tell them which programs have what advantages compared to other programs and to standards in the field. In teacher evaluation, a global summative evaluation tells the consumers or their representative which teachers are competent, excellent, or incompetent, and an analytical summative sets out the dimensions of their strengths and weaknesses. Hence the general requirement or expectation that summative evaluation should provide *either* recommendations about what to do *or* about how to improve the evaluand is simply indefensible. If we were to take this requirement seriously, it would mean that we should give up *Consumer Reports* and *Car & Driver* on the grounds that all they provide is analytical summative evaluation.

So recommendations for remediation are indeed very desirable, but an evaluation is not flawed if it fails to provide them. Even a doctor, whose job it is to prescribe a therapy where possible, cannot always do so. If he or she diagnoses terminal cancer, that is a diagnosis with evaluative content (the patient is seriously ill), but we can hardly fault it on the grounds that it is not accompanied by a suggestion for remediation. We can all agree that the situation in which therapeutic advice is appended is preferable, but its absence is not a sign of incompetent doctoring, only that medicine is not omnipotent. The situation is the same with proposals or programs. Sometimes recommendations naturally emerge from the evaluation process, but often they do not, and special and distinctly different expertise is needed to generate them. When evaluators are saddled with the expectation that they are to generate other results besides an evaluation, the evaluation effort is almost always deflected or diluted. It always involves extra cost and expertise. And it sometimes leads to resentment by decision makers who feel that their turf is being invaded by the evaluator.

The fault for this misconception lies not only at the door of the client. Evaluators are often attracted by the role of the Great Doctor when it is offered to them on a plate (although, in one field of evaluation, policy studies, the training of evaluators comes close to including the requisite remedial knowledge). Evaluators may also feel that they will lose too many clients if they opt out of the remedial aspect of the job, since client expectations are so strongly committed to including it.

If a client can find evaluators with all of the relevant expertise on both sides of the evaluative conclusion, so much the better; but more time is usually required to generate the recommendations. Often, it is better for clients to get the best evaluators and then use their own judgment, or get specialist advice, as to what to do in light of the results of the evaluation.

The importance of comparisons in evaluation (see Thesis 9) might suggest that the summative evaluator is at least always spinning off recommendations of the form "Buy car B rather than car A." But it is one thing to conclude that car B is better, and it is another to recommend that the client buy it. A demonstration of why it is better is part of the evaluation, but the decision to buy is often and justifiably controlled by factors that the evaluator serving a large audience cannot include, for example, the competence of the local dealership or whether the range of colors available includes a medium metallic green. The nearer an individual client, perhaps a single school, comes to providing all such factors and requesting that they be taken into account, the nearer the evaluator can, in principle, come to a recommendation. At the same time, the nearer one is asked to come to a recommendation, the broader the range of expertise and related data gathering skills needed, since local politics as well as personal factors are often a substantial part of the relevant ambience, and the extent to which this can be influenced or disregarded calls for a level of political savvy that few evaluators are in a position to claim.

In the limit, it is, of course, an evaluative task to determine the relative merits of the exact alternatives open to a client. But that usually is not the kind of evaluative task for which a professional evaluator is needed. Rather, a professional evaluator should be brought in to determine the relative merit of the items among which the client must choose, and to integrate that information with the details about local politics, funding sources, and so on with which the client is sure to be more familiar than is any outsider.

This position renders unto the evaluator much less turf than many commentators—and evaluators—have thought appropriate. But it should be borne in mind that many evaluators—from the weak decision support view to the constructivist view—argue for limiting the role of the evaluator to something that goes even less far toward meeting the requirements of the client. They have made the mistake of thinking that the line is appropriately drawn well short of evaluative conclusions. My position here is that the line should usually be drawn on the far side of the evaluative conclusions but the short side of recommendations, except when the recommendations happen to spin off from the evaluation's microanalysis ("The errors of fact in the safety manual should be corrected").

This chapter addresses a more sophisticated set of positions about program evaluation, all of which have been held by leading schools of thought in program evaluation at one time or another. The residue from these positions still is found in or widely supported by some departments and many professional evaluators.

Implications for Popular Models of Program Evaluation

In Chapter Two, I focused on the differences among widespread practices in program evaluation. In this chapter, I add details on the differences between the view supported in this volume and the views of other program evaluation theorists. My aim here is to clarify that the position advocated is not completely banal, regardless of whether it is sound.

Thesis 8: Pure outcome evaluation usually yields too little too late, and pure process evaluation is usually invalid or premature

The pure outcome or black-box model of evaluation is sometimes advocated as a desirable approach, usually on the grounds that it focuses on "what really matters," the results. It has the great merit of discouraging us from putting too much emphasis on the process, that is, on secondary indicators (which are only empirically correlated with the criterion variable, rather than part of it), when the real thing is available. However, this model is rarely ideal, partly because it ignores seriously improper practices in the workings of the program, and partly because it can usually only produce results too late. A good example, which is relevant to science, mathematics, engineering, and technology (SMET) education programs, concerns the suggestion that teachers should be evaluated on the basis of the performance of their former students, ten or twenty years downstream. Even if the logistical obstacles could be overcome, the utility of the results is near zero, since they relate to the performance of individuals who may have been incompetent then but are outstanding now; or excellent then, and burnt-out now.[26] The same, of course, applies to programs.

A pure process approach is equally flawed, although very popular, in other quarters. The standard procedure for evaluating teachers is a pure process approach, based on observations made during classroom visits. It is based on assumptions about the connection between what occurs in the classroom and what the learning gains of the students will be. These assumptions are based on very weak correlations in the best of circumstances, but even if they were strong correlations, to use them is to be guilty of judging someone by the performance of others who resemble them in some visible way, the same kind of error involved in racial or gender stereotyping. The obligation in personnel evaluation is to judge people on the basis of what they actually achieve, not what others who use their approach achieve. There are many ways to get a handle on the amount and value of the learning that takes place—the outcome component—and those factors must be given substantial weight in any legitimate process of teacher evaluation.

The compromise between process and outcomes evaluation involves looking at process for violations of absolute values, but not for indicators, which are substitutes for outcomes measures, when the latter are available. In formative evaluation, we might go a little further and mention alternative approaches to process that have tended to work a little better in general than those employed in the target case, but this procedure has no more evaluative status than that of suggestions.

Thesis 9: Noncomparative evaluations are comparatively useless

Lee Cronbach was the great advocate of avoiding comparative evaluation, and he may well have been reacting to excessive emphasis on inappropriate comparisons, such as overemphasis on norm-referenced student testing. The move to mastery approaches (that is, to grading instead of ranking) made excellent sense for certain purposes. But even in those cases, it is helpful to parents and students to also know how a student stands against others because there is no way to avoid, nor can there ever be any way to avoid, selection by merit for certain valuable limited resources, for example, scholarships, positions in the better colleges and with the best employers, and promotions once employed.[27]

In the program evaluation area, I have already set out the main arguments for the almost universal necessity to do comparative evaluations. There are also some dimensions along which one must do "absolute evaluation," including ethical, legal, and content accuracy dimensions, but they rarely constitute all that needs to be considered.

So, too, I have mentioned the reasons for having an "el cheapo" entry in the list of critical competitors. It is often worth keeping in mind the possibility of adding an "el magnifico" entry. This is an entry that costs more but offers much more than the difference in cost. How can we ever justify claims about "offering much more"? The reference here is, of course, to the trade-off between money and benefits (such as breadth or depth of learning) that is determined by the provider's resources and the recipient's needs. This is not a precise notion, but it is surely sensible, with many clear cases of correct application. For example, if it will cost us 20 percent more to get computers with multimedia capability for classroom use (the "el magnifico" option), but these computers will make it possible to offer fluent bilingual instruction in computer literacy and other subject matter, coverage that we cannot provide in any other way, then the extra investment may be a great bargain for us.

Thesis 10: Formative evaluation is attractive, but summative evaluation is imperative

In the history of evaluation theory, Cronbach is also well known for another salient position—the view that formative evaluation is (much) more important than summative evaluation. This is a kinder, gentler view, but unrealistic, and enough has been said already to condemn it. Every nonrandom decision rests on summative evaluation, and many such decisions are life saving, life threatening, or radically life enhancing, whether they occur in drug evaluation or the evaluation of weapons systems and aircraft, or guide investment in and regulation of business or government. Hence the process of improving the quality of those evaluations is a way to very large gains. In fact, hundreds of thousands of lives are saved or massively improved every day because decisions that affect them were based on good summative evaluation of the options, whether drugs, surgery, crime control, food, jobs, war, or major purchases were at issue. While life-and-death matters can hinge on good summative evaluation, however, we would only have fewer good options to choose among if there were no formative evaluation. Even if perfect formative evaluation were to be done by every educator, manager, manufacturer, and vendor, perfect ethical character and unlimited resources and creativity and reliability of these individuals would still be necessary before we consumers could take the risk of abandoning summative evaluation. So the bottom line is that summative is essential and is rightly and usefully done on a colossal scale.

Nor should the other main reason for doing summative evaluations be discounted, namely, accountability, one of the tasks of federal regulatory and supervisory agencies, and not one that taxpayers are likely to dismiss. Indeed, summative evaluation is arguably part of the ethical responsibility of government. Cronbach and others (1980, Thesis 18) do not think very much of this task: "A demand for accountability is a sign of pathology in the political system." But it is also one way to avoid pathology in the political system.

Related to accountability is the question of efficiency, one of the criteria used in many program evaluations and surely a sensible criterion to consider. Cronbach and others (1980, Thesis 20) have a similar degree of enthusiasm for this concept: "The ideal of efficiency in government is in tension with the ideal of democratic participation." Indeed, it turns out that they see something sinister about even the more basic notion of rationalism: "Rationalism is dangerously close to totalitarianism." Both claims seem naive now. At the surface level, Cronbach and his colleagues seem naive for their distaste for what is common sense in every applied field of evaluation: a concern for efficiency. But they are also naive at a deeper level because, to take the first quotation as an example, if one thinks that there are good practical arguments for democracy as a form of government, it would be self-contradictory to define efficiency in government in a way that excludes democratic participation. Indeed, it is hard to find conceptions of efficiency so simplistic as to ignore long-term consequences such as revolutions and short-term problems such as program failure because of lack of input from the recipients of the services provided. But these are some of the results that we get if we reject democratic participation. It seems a little inefficient to ignore them. (Of course, there is an ethical element in democracy to which we would also appeal as a constraint on any conception of efficiency that we were going to implement.)

Similarly, if one thinks that there are good, rational arguments against totalitarianism, then rationalism can hardly be a kissing cousin of totalitarianism. The cited remarks of Cronbach and his colleagues intimate a lingering hankering for the values-free doctrine, for they have continued to suppose that there is some kind of logical gulf between the domain of reason and that of value, that is, that the domain of reason cannot provide support for arrangements such as democratic participation.

No doubt, formative evaluation is of vast importance in making the world a better place. It provides us with the guidance that we need to improve the world directly. Done well, it prevents disaster for many consumers who lack the resources to do summative evaluation of the resulting products. But this hardly justifies Cronbach and others' (1980, p. 62) conclusion: "Evaluations are used almost entirely in a formative manner when they *are* used." Difficult funding decisions, at the micro- and macrolevels, and accountability considerations have generated many (summative) evaluations, and the evaluations have led to many major decisions about future funding.[28]

Thus, the fact that Cronbach and his colleagues were talking about program evaluation, not evaluation in general, hardly makes their conclusion plausible.[29] Looking back on the history of SMET programs, we can see that many of them got their start from a band of enthusiasts and came to a halt because of the cold shock of evaluations, often much later than they should have. Outside the main SMET area, but within the area of education programs, "Sesame Street," one of the great educational phenomena of the last twenty years, got its start from the favorable Educational Testing Service evaluation. Since the evaluation was crucially invalid and in no way established the effectiveness of the program, as Tom Cook and others showed later, this is not an example of which evaluators should be proud; but anyone who talks regularly and extensively with school personnel will learn that the evaluation is what produced their support. The rebirth of Head Start also appears to have been fueled by new evaluation results. And so on.

Cronbach and his colleagues may have been misled, as have many other evaluators, by the lag between evaluation reports and the acceptance of their conclusions. Politics provides a massive buffer between truth and action. But people tend to come around to the truth; and as personnel change, the power of the "not invented here" taboo is added to the results of negative evaluations and often leads to the death of programs that should have been killed earlier. It is unfortunately true that the power of the National Institutes of Health can overcome even favorable evaluations, but no one is arguing for the actual supremacy of evaluation over all political and psychological forces.

The argument for formative evaluation, like that for summative, is so strong that any attempt to rank them seems misguided. Both involve the same logic: Formative is only essentially different in that it occurs earlier, while it can still be used to improve the program, and is delivered to those who can still improve the program instead of to those who have to make some decision about the program. If possible, one tries to do formative in a way that makes it easier to identify the places where change is most needed, provided that such an effort does not weaken the basic design, that is, one tries for analytical formative. If possible, one samples the space of users and uses with an emphasis on the data points that are most likely to cause big trouble or yield big payoffs, because those are the points where one wants to be sure that the program has been bulletproofed. But doing this kind of analysis is a bonus, usually an expensive addition, not part of the essential nature of formative evaluation. What formative evaluation must cover is the basis for an early-warning summative. And that achievement alone can still serve the formative purpose very well, although not as well as would be possible with more resources to answer the microquestions that developers would like to have answered.

To serve as early-warning summative evaluation, valid formative evaluation must incorporate the essence of summative, whether or not summative is ever done. And summative, in a way, is just formative done too late to help improve the program—it is life after death for formative. These are complementary, not competing, activities.[30]

Thesis 11: Rich description is not an approach to program evaluation but a retreat from it

One can see the development of sophisticated program evaluation as a series of swings away from one or the other of the twin terrors that have always dominated our thought about evaluation, in everyday life as well as in the disciplines. The mental paralysis that these terrors induce has led to the schizophrenia of the "values-free evaluation" practiced by social scientists in our time, just as surely as it led to the moral inconsistency in the story of the Garden of Eden, where Adam and Eve are punished for acquiring knowledge of good and evil, in the absence of which they could not be culpable. On the one hand, there is the fear of being judgmental and incurring the wrath of those whom we judge. On the other hand, there is the fear of being indiscriminate and totally tolerant; this is the relativism of those who think that ethics is a set of conventions comparable to the rules of driving, and the beliefs that to understand everything is to forgive everything.

In program evaluation, these two schools are unequally represented, in reverse proportions to their representation in product evaluation, where calibrated judgment is thoroughly acceptable. The majority group in program evaluation is composed of de facto relativists, the social scientists who explicitly bought the values-free doctrine, while refuting it implicitly with their everyday practice as scientists and teachers of science. Several smaller groups have developed general theories to accommodate this kind of values-free or devalued evaluation, and Thesis 11 denounces one set of these approaches, just as Thesis 12 denounces a more radical set who are also overreacting to the horrors of the judgmental role.

The rich description approach (the latest variant is "thick description," perhaps because it sounds less evaluative) is here grouped with the naturalistic approach, the ethnographic model, transactional evaluation, and the connoisseurship model. It seems hard to avoid the conclusion that this kind of approach is essentially escapist and unrealistic. This is a world in which hard choices have to be made, and the metachoice is only between making them well and making them badly. Evaluation should be seen as a way to help make them well, not as a way to avoid making them. The rich description approach substitutes detailed observations for evaluation and passes the buck of evaluation back to the client after doing some fancy embroidering on it. The approach is analogous to a physician who runs all of the office tests on a patient, orders all of the laboratory tests and X rays, and then gives the printouts to the patient. It is the doctor's job to interpret as well as test, and give the patient the synthesis. Provision of just the data, synthesized in the usual technical ways, simply produces the response, "Well, but what does all this add up to?" That is the hard question; data gathering and number crunching are just the first steps toward evaluation.

In personnel evaluation, something like the rich description approach is exemplified at the University of California at Santa Cruz, where the usual grade transcript has been replaced with essays about each student, written by a committee of his or her teachers. About all one can say is that this approach gets the authors out of the frying pan of grading and into the fire of essay writing; at Santa Cruz, they think that the fire is cooler. But at the receiving end, it is a bad deal. What does the graduate school admissions committee do with all of this prose? Convert it into grades, of course, literally or mentally. What else are they going to do when they have to rank the applicants from Santa Cruz with those from other schools? Moreover, they presumably make the condensation less well than the student's original teachers could have done. Those who think that they can better match the student to their program by reading essays presumably know little about the research on the subjectivity of this process.

Is Santa Cruz just an example of giving in to bad practices because everyone does it? The idea that the world would be a better place if every college did what Santa Cruz did is right in there with the idea that we should abandon descriptive statistics in favor of raw data. The real world uses grades and grade point averages for the same reasons that it uses the statistical averages of means, medians, and modes, not just because there is not time to read the raw data on which they are based but because they are more meaningful and intellectually more manageable (more easily manipulable), and their use leads to fewer errors if they are used for the purposes for which they are suited. The problem is not that Santa Cruz is out of step. If every college submitted essays instead of grade point averages, the comparisons of candidates on the basis of these descriptions would be even more subjective than they are now, and so they would probably all have to be reduced to some variation of grade point averages in an unreliable way.

Grades are second-order data summaries, integrating a set of standards or requirements (for example, needs or legal standards) with performance data; we use them for the same kind of reason that we use statistics and theoretical constructs, because there is no alternative that works nearly as well. Of course, these summaries throw away masses of the information content of the original. But it is also true that, compiled reasonably well, they add information content of a kind that we need. The act of synthesis required to produce them creates information that was not visible before, for any user. Thus, for many purposes, they convey more of the truth, in needed respects and with greater reliability, than does perusal of raw data. Grading is one of the ultimate forms of data compression; a whole year's work can be compressed into a single letter grade. Only dreamers in the ivory tower bemoan this procedure; the proof that they are only dreamers is that while bemoaning it, they use it every time they read a consumer's digest before buying something. Of course, grades must be used with care given their limitations; as must averages, as must theories, as must tests.

The Santa Cruz essays are also evaluative; they simply avoid letter grades. Hence they are not quite analogous to the rich description approach that is supposed to avoid evaluative language. But the same argument applies a fortiori to the rich descriptions: They are even further from the kind of analysis that the consumer needs.

The National Science Foundation has had substantial experience with "responsive evaluation," a variation of rich description favored by Robert Stake and applied by him to the evaluation of a major science education program. One must treat Stake very seriously. He is the Picasso of modern evaluation theory. He used to do a more traditional form of it very well and so has demonstrated all of the technical skills. That rules out the possibility that he is going the soft-hearted route because he cannot do it the hard way. He is not the only program evaluator to make a midlife switch away from evaluation; C. West Churchman, of operations research fame, did the same. However, there are other reasons for becoming less engagé in one's later years, and one needs to look carefully at the explicit arguments as well as at examples before abandoning the seemingly serviceable but supposedly simple-minded view of evaluation as a process of working out what works well or best (see Thesis 29).

The best use of the rich description approach is as a supplement to more traditional methods. In the National Science Foundation study, that was its role. When the time came to synthesize the results, people more frequently quoted material from the rich description component than from any other. That illustrates not only its utility in making the numbers meaningful (the good news) but also the traps of graphical material (the bad news). Graphical description can often have more influence than it deserves because of its newsbyte power to capture the imagination. An ethnographic approach can involve richness, comparative studies, interpretation, synthesis, and so on, but it cannot provide a firm grip on the generalizability of the differences, and of a dozen other aspects of the program that require proactive investigation and analysis. Both elements are needed.

Thesis 12: One can only attain fourth-generation evaluation by counting backward

The most radical of the relativists, those who wish to deny the legitimacy of all evaluative conclusions, are typified by Guba and Lincoln, whose work is the most frequently published among this group. In *Fourth Generation Evaluation* (Guba and Lincoln, 1989), they introduced the title term by saying that it involves going beyond the first three generations in evaluation, which they characterize as "measurement-oriented, description-oriented, and judgment-oriented" on "to a new level whose key dynamic is *negotiation*" (p. 8). Their position begins with the view that evaluations do not report on any objective truth but rather represent the result of negotiations.

One problem with the negotiation approach is that it blends the evaluator's role into the manager's role, since the negotiations are with the program staff. We have seen that type of confusion before, in supposing that the evaluator is an automatic source of recommendations (the manager's job), or in thinking that the evaluator's job is just to tell the manager how well the program is going toward its target (the manager's target). The problem here is to decide who gets to be in on the negotiation, and whether we substitute a power struggle, or even a friendly division of plunder, for an ethical process based on factual premises.

In his article in *The Paradigm Dialog* (Guba, 1990), whose title also refers to the need for a fundamentally new conception of evaluation, Dennis Phillips has pointed out the essential flaw in the negotiation approach, namely, its supporters are obliged to deny the legitimacy of all standards of truth, not just the standards of truth for evaluation. That is not the case with the rich description approach, or the kind of negotiation involved in the approach articulated by Cronbach and others (1980). But the new constructionists, Egon Guba, for example, in taking an extra step in the same direction, are precipitated into an epistemological skepticism that would force us back to the days before there was anything that could be regarded as measurement, hence the phrase "counting backward" in Thesis 12.

This chapter begins to refine the concepts and processes involved in evaluation design. For example, it moves from generic evaluation designs to specific designs depending on whether a ranking, a grading, or an apportioning is required. And it gives proper place to synthesis, which is so often done impressionistically or not done at all.

Intermediate Evaluation Design Issues

Here, I introduce substantive conceptual issues that affect program evaluation design in fundamental ways, although I do little more than explain them briefly and illustrate them with an example or two. They show something of the content of the core discipline of evaluation and are applicable to program evaluation as well as to every other branch of evaluation.

Thesis 13: Merit and quality are not the same as worth or value

Evaluation is a process of determining certain evaluable properties of things, but there is more than one kind of such properties. Perhaps the most fundamental and important distinction among them is between merit or quality and worth or value. It may be easiest to see this distinction in a case from personnel evaluation, specifically, teacher evaluation. The merit of teachers is a matter of how well they teach whatever it is that they teach. Suppose the best teacher in a high school teaches French. Suppose that enrollments in the French courses decline because of a shift away from languages in general and a shift within languages toward Spanish and away from French. Eventually, it becomes clear that this teacher will have to be let go. He or she has not declined in merit. What has changed is that the teacher's worth or value to the school has evaporated. Worth or value in this context means benefit to the institution, the meeting of needs; merit means quality according to the standards of the profession.

    The same distinction applies across most fields of evaluation. The new S-series Mercedes is a fine car by the standards of cars, that is, it has merit; but with prices starting at over $80,000 and a fuel efficiency level at about eleven miles per gallon, it does not represent a good value—for almost anyone and for society as a whole—because of the competition from the BMW 7-series and the Lexus LS 400 and Infiniti Q45. The latter two cars are at about half the price of the Mercedes and match or surpass it on essentially every dimension except perhaps prestige among the ecologically insensitive (they get between 60 percent and 90 percent better mileage).

Looking at programs, we can see the same distinction. It is related to but broader than the difference between effectiveness and efficiency, which is close to the difference between evaluation with and without attention to cost analysis. In evaluation design and critique, and even in program design, one must determine whether merit or worth is the focus. It was because that distinction was not made at the start that we spent so much money so pointlessly on some of the more lavish New Math programs.

Thesis 14: Different evaluation designs are usually required for ranking, grading, scoring, and apportioning

Looking more closely still at evaluation design, we can see that, in general, each of the evaluative predicates requires a different design. Evaluation is normally aimed at a conclusion that is expressed in terms of ranking, grading (or rating), scoring, or apportioning (distributing valuable resources). For example, a foot race or a horse race produces a ranking without a rating. Recorded observations of the intervals between consecutive runners as they cross the finish line adds a primitive type of scoring ("won by inches," "third by a length," and so on). A stopwatch provides a kind of scoring that makes grading possible ("world class" versus "nothing to write home about"). In program evaluation, we are often interested in both ranking and rating; for decision making, we normally need scoring as well, because only scoring gives us the size of the difference. Were we to look at many large-scale evaluation designs, especially those of the 1970s, we would notice that they fail to focus on this issue, which leads either to a failure to answer the key question or to a very expensive way to answer it. (In technical language, the reference here is to the need for interval scales rather than mere ordinal scales; it is hard to find cases where a ratio scale is of much practical importance in evaluation.)

This point has two consequences of particular interest to agency staff. First, it is acutely relevant to proposal evaluation. Panels should never be asked to give full rankings of proposals if all that is necessary are ratings ("Definitely fund" or "Definitely do not fund") and a ranking for borderline cases only. A great deal more work is involved in ranking; maximum accuracy requires something close to pairwise comparisons of all possible pairs. Usually, the reason given for requiring a ranking is that the proposals recommended (or rejected) for funding may not all be acceptable for political reasons, and the ranking below the cutting point is necessary to facilitate any needed "dipping" to match geographical or minority quotas and so on. More careful thought about the extent of this problem and appropriate solutions can result in substantial savings of panel time and costs (see Thesis 19).

Second, apportionment is important to agency policy, such as when there is not enough money to go around and programs have to be cut back. The algorithm for apportioning has been discussed in the literature and avoids primitive approaches such as across-the-board cuts. The latter approach rewards those who inflate their budgets and encourages everyone to inflate budgets for next year's exercise; the apparent evenhandedness is entirely illusory. Nor is the process of ranking and then funding from the top down acceptable; nor are any combinations of these. The correct solution is a solution to the so-called portfolio problem of the investment consultant, as Nick Smith has pointed out, and is connected to an extended use of the concept of marginal utility and to zero-based budgeting.[31]

Thesis 15: Needs assessments provide some but not all of the values needed for evaluations

This point was developed in the course of supporting Thesis 1. The leading considerations in addition to needs are the so-called absolute values of ethics, truth, and so on, the social values embodied in law and politics, the logical values discovered from conceptual analysis, and sometimes just the preferences of the affected population—the wants rather than the needs, when no needs supervene or remain to be satisfied. Even the current extended sense of needs assessment is not explicitly unpacked to cover all of these values, but all of them must be at least scanned in the course of evaluation.

Thesis 16: Money costs are hard to determine—but they are the easy part of cost analysis

Money cost analyses are not just associated with input but must be done for outcomes, since the latter often include cost recovery. We have looked at this point briefly already, where I stressed that the psychological and political costs as well as other, more conventional, nonmoney costs, for example, space, time, environment, and expertise, often override all monetary considerations. It should also be noted that the usual definition of cost in economics texts is fallacious—that is, it is equated with opportunity cost—and so one must consider opportunity cost separately from other costs.

Thesis 17: Program evaluation should begin with the presuppositions of the program and sometimes go no further

This point addresses some of the truth in the deconstructionist and constructivist approaches and in other approaches that stress the need for analysis of the social context in which evaluation is done (for example, House, 1980). But it avoids the fourth-generation mistake of going overboard on the epistemological implications of the discovery of fundamental bias and thus undermining the insights by attacking the foundations of all truth. Presuppositions, like assumptions, are sometimes implicit, other times stated.

In my original draft of the discussion here, I developed in detail an example of each type of presupposition, taken from the area of science, mathematics, engineering, and technology (SMET) education programs. One was the absence of the concept of evaluation from all lists of key scientific concepts that form the basis for the new science curricula of the past thirty years. Another was the absence from the school curriculum of any treatment of technology as an autonomous discipline, whereas in fact it shares none of the goals or training required for science. Due to space restrictions, I again can mention a third example only in passing: Many SMET programs have been built on the results of standardized testing, but the National Science Foundation-funded Boston College study found that these tests have been giving us a massively biased picture of the state of student learning in mathematics and science. Moreover, their effect on the teaching of these subjects has been in the opposite direction from most of our efforts to reform science and mathematics teaching. Here again a presupposition has let us down.

Thesis 18: Establishing statistical significance is the easy part of establishing significance

It was not so very long ago, in the early days of program evaluation, that the shadow of pseudoscience obscured the truth in much evaluation. It is still a weakness in the "social science model" of evaluation. A classic example is the long history of treating statistical significance as if it were the precise scientific version of an imprecise everyday notion of significance (see Morrison and Henkel, 1970; Scriven, 1988). The analogy that dominated thought about this was the way in which the thermodynamic definition of temperature replaced the less precise everyday notion. However, there are several dimensions to the everyday concept of significance, and only one of them relates to the question of whether results are unlikely to have occurred by chance. Results that are real and not statistical artifacts may be completely lacking in significance. For example, they may have been so costly to obtain as to have no interest for any other user, or they may be of such a small size as to be insignificant as a contribution to a large problem.

Thus, the "Sesame Street" evaluation, even though biased in the direction of positive results, only established a trivial difference between the experimental and control groups; but the size of these groups was so large—thousands of pupils—that this tiny difference was statistically significant, and in favor of the group viewing the program. It was a real difference, but for $7 million it was truly insignificant. Yet, the evaluation report did not mention the absolute size of the difference; it only gave the extent of the statistical significance. In those days, and perhaps even now among many people, that was the only catchet that counted.

Size is one way to statistical significance, but it often gets in the way of good evaluation and good development. Cronbach and others (1980, p. 9) have expressed the point well in their Thesis 77: "Large-scale evaluations are not necessarily better than smaller ones." Today, there are many who would say that a set of well-planned, well-developed, and well-followed-up small evaluations is almost certainly better than a large-scale evaluation of a multisite project.

If we are interested in real significance, we ignore little differences such as in the "Sesame Street" case for another reason besides their negligible cost-effectiveness. We ignore them because, although they are very likely real, they are very unlikely to hold up in replications. Fred Mosteller, the great applied statistician, was fond of saying that he did not care much for statistically significant differences, he was more interested in interocular differences, the differences that hit us between the eyes. He thought that the function of statistical significance was to help identify the effects that might be refined to the point where they showed really significant, that is, interocular, differences.

Another way of approaching the significance issue is via the notion of critical competitors. A program is not of much significance, no matter how well it does, if we can do considerably better for less. How could we do better than "Sesame Street"? For $7 million (which were just the direct costs) we could do much better. The crudest alternative would be to select the students with the worst reading problems and give them tutors, who would work with just one or two or three students at a time. Or we could use programmed texts of proven power: the Sullivan readers. In order to compete with the durability of "Sesame Street," the latter approach, especially if systematically based on what happened with the tutorial work, would have the advantage. But the former approach would probably still beat "Sesame Street" in terms of significant changes in the lives of large numbers of children.

So, with large amounts of quantitative data, the task of getting the probability value into the significance stratosphere is the easy part, just one of many hurdles that we need to clear. And sometimes it is not necessary to clear that hurdle because results can be shown to be real without using statistics. The use of more sophisticated statistics and of measures such as effect size helps a little, but it still leaves out the key currency—the needs assessment. Only when we can cut an appreciable slice out of the needs do we have something significant. And the need in education is not just for a way to teach reading but a way to teach reading at an affordable cost.

Of course, the statistical test is also completely worthless if the data are not representative and comprehensive. And statistical significance is useless in the tricky cases that have recently emerged in personnel evaluation, essentially because it is usually improper to use statistical indicators when evaluating individuals. Even characteristics that are highly correlated with job-relevant performance cannot be used for personnel evaluation, for scientific reasons that are quite sufficient even if the legal and ethical ones did not apply. It is not enough to know that blue-eyed brunettes are almost all thieves; we should not give blue eyes and brown hair any nonzero weight at all when judging the merit of an individual candidate, regardless of ethics.[32] Essentially, all current teacher evaluation procedures and the use of almost any "empirically validated" psychological test involves just that fallacy.[33] Only a broad-based discipline of evaluation can provide the perspective necessary to recognize fallacies of this kind.

We have been conned by the quantifiers, and in fact they conned themselves. By getting evaluation into shape as a discipline, we can help ourselves avoid statistical scams.

Thesis 19: "Pulling it all together" is where most evaluations fall apart

Most of us have tried to address major purchasing, hiring, or career decisions in our lives in a systematic way. The intuitive approach is to list the criteria of merit (needs, wants, and other relevant values) in a column down the left-hand side of a page, and the candidates across the top. Many people go a step further to make this into a quantitative approach. In an extra column next to the first column that lists the merit criteria, they enter a weight to indicate the importance of each criterion, perhaps a number from 1 to 5 or 1 to 10. In the remaining cells on each row, they enter numbers to indicate the performances of the various candidates on that criterion, perhaps a number from 1 to 10 or 1 to 100. Then they multiply each performance by its weight and sum the result at the bottom of each column to get a total weighted performance score for each candidate—and the candidate with the best score is the winner. Apart from its personal use, this is a model for the integration stage in any complex evaluation, where we are pulling together the scores of a program on each dimension that we are considering.

This happens to be an invalid model, and innumerable errors in personal decision making as well as personnel selection, program evaluation, and so on have resulted from its use. That this model is invalid is significant enough, but the more important fact is that it took so long to detect the invalidity. Lost time and effort constitute one of the truly serious costs of not taking evaluation seriously, hence not looking at its procedures with a critical eye.[34]

At least the approach just described is algorithmic, hence it provides a checkable model, although checking it is very difficult. To an astonishing degree, program and personnel evaluations involving very large costs and benefits leave the integration stage open to impressionistic interpretation of a large matrix of ratings (or even raw scores) or, still worse, the rich description substitute. The approach described—the numerical weight-and-sum approach (NWS)—does reduce the unreliability errors that occur in the informal approach, with offers too much opportunity for a kind of inkblot projection of one's own preferences on the data. Its problems focus on the following key difficulty. It is not possible to find a range for the weighting scale and a range for the performance scale that avoid distortion of their intent by the number of criteria, a number that we cannot anteced-ently determine—or even fix at any point in an evaluation, since new criteria frequently emerge—and that can range from four or five to two hundred in common practical evaluation problems. Running scores of parallel evaluations, using different weighting and performance scales, show that the NWS approach will usually not give good approximations to the correct answer.

The correct answer can only be obtained by weakening the (naive) scaling assumptions of NWS. (One cannot reasonably assume that a single scale can be used for importance, performance, and number of criteria; and without the single scale, the multiply-and-compare step will not work.) This action automatically destroys the possibility of an algorithm. The preliminary solution that I have proposed, qualitative weight and sum (QWS), leaves us with heuristics that can handle all cases, but not so conveniently (and, of course, my approach may be invalid; see Scriven, 1991). So it is important for program evaluators to understand the prob-lems with impressionistic synthesis, NWS, and QWS.

Two brief comments about the synthesis process are warranted. First, naive academics often exclaim with consternation that an evaluation problem, say, that of deciding which one of two totally different programs to fund, is "like comparing apples with oranges." Most evaluation involves doing just that, and the analogy is interesting because everyone going to the produce market is entirely used to comparing apples and oranges when they want some fruit. They pick one kind or a mix (apportionment) on the basis of one or several of the criteria that apply to both kinds of fruit, for example, cost, quality, nutrition, and appearance, and they synthesize these quite readily and properly. Of course, many academic decisions involve exactly the same kind of comparison, for example, the college of engineering can either upgrade the materials testing laboratory or lease time on a Cray, and they will often use some variant of NWS to decide. But the academic culture in general has not caught up with the analysis of its own serious thinking in the evaluation area.

Second, we have so far skated quickly over the extent to which the chain of inference from raw data to an evaluative conclusion involves several levels of evaluative integration. What we finally integrate is often not measurements but subevaluations (for example, ratings), which we obtained by integrating measurements or lower-level subevaluations. Hence the synthesis process can be a key element throughout an evaluation, not just at the end, which is all the more reason for understanding what it involves and how it can be improved. One question that naturally arises is, Where do the weights come from in program evaluation? The answer again is from the needs assessment or all-relevant-values search.

This short chapter addresses the issue of the credibility and utility of evaluations, considerations which go beyond validity.

An Advanced Evaluation Design Issue: Beyond Validity

Theses 20 and 21 in this chapter had to be reduced to titles only, in the interest of text reduction. Most of the supporting text is inferrable from prior material and the discussion presented in support of Thesis 22.

Thesis 20: Validity does not ensure credibility

Thesis 21: Validity and credibility do not ensure utility

Thesis 22: Even utilization does not ensure utility

There has been a great deal of discussion in the evaluation literature about increasing what is seen as an excessively low level of utilization of evaluation results. It seems likely that much of this concern is misplaced. An indication of one kind of mistake in the discussion is the quite frequent use of the phrase "lack of implementation" instead of "lack of utilization." Implementation only applies to recommendations, and for reasons given earlier, recommendations are not something that evaluations should automatically generate.

If the evaluation only generates evaluative conclusions, it is not clear that one can readily tell what counts as "utilization." It would be necessary to see what effect it had on opinion among the decision makers who received it, a notoriously difficult matter to establish through interviews because it is not clear just what action should follow acceptance of an evaluative conclusion. This will rightly depend very much on the circumstances. Take an example from product evaluation. I may go to considerable trouble and expense to acquire a competent evaluation of one of the new palm-top computers, because I am seriously interested in buying one. I get the evaluation as a download from an online data base maintained by Ziff-Davis, read it carefully, and do (or do not) buy the computer. As is often the case, the evaluation says some good things and some bad things about the product; it might conclude—the nearest that it is likely to get to a recommendation—by noting that this item would be useful for people with certain needs, and not for those with different needs. When interviewed later by a representative of Ziff-Davis who is doing a market survey, I say that the evaluation was very useful in making my decision. But if observers of this sequence of events are dubious that I was just being nice to a representative of the staff who did the evaluation, and they try to make sure that I told the truth by observing my purchasing behavior, they face the problem that no specific behavior can be tied to the influence, since either purchase or nonpurchase might result from reading the evaluation. It seems possible that people who have been concerned about utilization of evaluations have too simple an idea of the connection between utility and action.

From some of the discussion in the evaluation literature, it also appears they are attracted by the idea that simple self-protection is the main reason why managers do not do just what the evaluator thought they should do. I have no idea whether or not this claim is true, but one certainly cannot jump to it as if it is the only explanation of nonacceptance. There are a dozen other good explanations, and unless they are ruled out, it is premature to take the cynical view.

Even if an evaluation is used, this does not establish that it was useful (had utility), only that it was usable. *Useful* is an endorsement, a favorable (meta-)evaluation; *usable* is the property of qualifying for use and describes a minimal capability, an entry requirement. After we discover that an evaluation was used (the "Sesame Street" evaluation was used), there remains the question of whether the evaluation was valid (it was not) and the question of whether the way in which it was used was consistent with its content (it also was not). By contrast, the Writing-to-Read evaluation conducted by the Educational Testing Service was valid and also was improperly used to justify the program. So, many evaluations that are used should not have been used, and we should be concerned about the amount of use rather than its lack.

On the other hand, if an evaluation is not used, this may be because it was not addressed to the key questions facing the decision maker, or because it did not suit the prejudices of the decision maker, or because it was too hard to understand, or for a dozen other reasons that may or may not give us good grounds to be thankful that it was not used. So use is neither a necessary nor a sufficient condition for utility. One should focus a critical study of evaluation in practice not on utilization but rather on the quality of the evaluation, using, for example, the criteria of merit mentioned in Chapter Four.

It is, however, entirely proper to look hard at ways to increase the utility of an evaluation. We already have learned a good deal about this issue. The next thesis stresses one aspect of it.

Thesis 23: Program evaluation involves research and ends with a report, but research reports are negative paradigms for evaluation reports

In the early days of modern program evaluation, and even today, people used the term *evaluation research* to refer to what we have been discussing here as evaluation. It was part of the effort to show that program evaluation was applied social science. That effort has many unfortunate consequences, perhaps none so hard to shake off as the idea that an evaluation report should look something like a social science research report. There are indeed evaluation reports that are parts of a layered set, and evaluation reports that are undertaken simply because their authors intend to publish them in professional journals. But most of the evaluation reports that look like research reports should not look that way. That format is aimed at the social science peer group, with similar research interests and familiar with the jargon of the trade. The format is almost useless for most clients and audiences, even if they are professional researchers in some other discipline (for example, from the science, mathematics, engineering, and technology group). Evaluation reports are a whole new field of presentations by comparison with research reports. For example, they may be layered, that is, there may be several reports on the same project aimed at different audiences and varying in terminology, length, examples and analogies, graphics emphasis, and concerns addressed. They may be verbal rather than written; they may be on disk rather than on paper (because of the use of hypertext or search facilities); they may be finger pointing or exculpatory in emphasis (both fully correct); they may address entirely different contrasts or options. In short, reports should avoid the appearance of research reports unless there are special reasons for using the latter format. And they should always be based on careful thought or even research about the audiences to whom they are addressed.

*This chapter addresses a major problem of practical methodology—
the problem of bias control and the pervasive threat of general positive
bias.*

An Advanced Evaluation
Management Issue: Bias Control

We have already considered what are partly management issues, some of
them under the heading of credibility. Here, I pick up another thread,
referring to what is perhaps the most widely misunderstood concept in
panel management, the issue of bias.

Thesis 24: Preference and commitment do not entail bias

It is crucial to begin with a clear idea of the difference between bias in the
sense of prejudice, which means a tendency to error, and bias in the
(sloppy) sense of preference, support, endorsement, acceptance, or favoring of one side of an issue. Only the first of these senses is derogatory, and
in the legal context the term bias is restricted to the first sense. From none
of the synonyms for the second sense can one infer prejudice, because the
preference, support, and so on may be justified. It is insulting, and never
tolerated in a court of law where these matters are of the essence, to treat
someone who has preferences as if they are thereby biased (and hence not
a fair witness). It is especially absurd in the science, mathematics, engineering, and technology (SMET) area to act as if belief in, for example, the
heliocentric arrangement of the universe shows bias. Bias must be shown,
either by demonstrating a pattern of error or by demonstrating the pres-
ence of an attitude that definitely and regularly produces error. Certainly,
a bigoted attitude wrought from what everyone thinks are true beliefs tends
to produce intolerance and hence error in dealing with evidence that the
time has come to change those beliefs; but the mere possession of the
beliefs does not show that one is intolerant of evidence concerning their
falsity. We may overrate the extent to which scientists have a genuine
scientific attitude, that is, they may not be infallibly open-minded, but we

NEW DIRECTIONS FOR PROGRAM EVALUATION, no. 58, Summer 1993 © Jossey-Bass Publishers have no reason to suppose that they are never or almost never willing to be fair in judging evidence that counts against their current beliefs. Science could not exist if this were true.

False beliefs imply other erroneous beliefs, but true beliefs do not. Having an opinion on a matter does not tend to produce error unless an individual, like some of the deconstructionists, cannot distinguish truth from error. The National Institutes of Health recently showed complete confusion about this difference when they switched a panelist to nonvoting status because of his well-known views about a matter on which his panel was to vote. People with knowledge about an area are typically people with views about it; the way to avoid panels of ignoramuses or compulsive fence sitters is to go for a balance of views, not an absence of views.

Thesis 25: The usual agency counsel's criteria for avoidance of conflict of interest select for ignorance, low contributions, indecisiveness, or some combination thereof

Courts of law are clear about the distinction between bias and preference, but attorneys are often biased about it. This comes up in dealing with conflict of interest, a major source of bias. Asking agency counsel for an opinion about a possible conflict of interest in a panelist is like asking a security officer whether a candidate is a security risk. The situation of the security officer is "all downside risk," as the analysts of a different kind of security are prone to say; that is, if they clear someone who later turns out to be corrupt, they are likely to get in trouble; whereas if they fail someone who is not in fact corrupt, no one will notice. Both the attorney and the Federal Bureau of Investigation agent are therefore under considerable pressure (retention of their jobs) to be fail-safe, that is, they have a strong bias toward false positives, namely, false identification of conflict and security risk, respectively.

A typical conflict-of-interest case entails a contract to be let for a program or evaluation, and the panelists are asked to reveal previous associations, including short-term consulting, with any of the bidders. Learned counsel for some agencies has in the past simply kicked such people off the panel, with the pathetic result, in certain areas, that most people with an adequate knowledge of what it takes to manage a large program in those areas are ruled ineligible because the only way they could acquire that knowledge was by working with one of the few players. Now that is confused. The counsel assumes that past connections carry over more strongly in the direction of bias than in the direction of increased expertise, an unfounded claim. Nor are considerations of credibility enough to salvage counsel's position here. People understand very well the need for relevant knowledge. They understand the commonsense solution: Rule out clear current or future financial or personal involvement of interest in panelists or their immediate families, balance the panel, but do not insist on panelists without preferences. After all, among those with preferences are some who are right, and many more who can contribute useful insights and arguments to the panel. We do not throw people out of Congress or Parliament because they are union members or antiunion, Democrats or Republicans, and so on. There would not be many people left. And Congress decides everything that affects us. We should not throw people off panels even if they are known to favor one point of view or candidate under consideration, as long as they have reasons for doing so, especially if they are balanced by others favoring the alternatives, let alone on the grounds that they once had something to do with a candidate.

In general, the commonsense and legally correct algorithm is, if one is an agency officer and on the verge of calling in agency counsel, do not bother—the candidate qualifies. If the conduct is not interocular, it is not significant.

Thesis 26: Program officers are biased toward favorable findings

We now turn to the great phenomenon of general positive bias and its version of the 80/20 rule, that is, 80 percent of all evaluations of new programs are generally favorable, whereas at most around 20 percent of new programs are, on balance, worthwhile.[35] I develop this point via a six-step historical exercise, reliving our development of acuity in the detection of bias.

First, would we, as agency program officers, ask program managers to author the only evaluations that we commission of their programs? Of course not. Why not? Probable bias and low credibility. Good answer. In the 1960s, that is how we evaluated many of our smaller programs. Of course, all the evaluations were positive. We have learned better.[36]

Second, we stipulated that the proposal must allocate 10 percent of the budget to the evaluation and that the evaluation was to be done by someone other than the program's own staff. Mistake. "Allocating in the proposal" does not mean "must be spent on." It turned out that the "substantial" part of the program always ran over budget, so the program managers never got to the evaluation part, which they cleverly figured they would put in at the end (great for getting baseline data). We got far fewer evaluations than under the first system, and not much evidence that the few that did come in were of any better quality.

Third, by the time of "Sesame Street," it was stipulated not only that a certain percentage of the budget must be used for an independent evaluation but also that a contract for that amount had to be let within a short period after the program was funded. For "Sesame Street," the evaluation contract was for one million dollars of the seven million total.

Better: but still fatally flawed. The evaluation contract was written and let by the program's manager and her staff. So she, for all that we can ensure back at the agency, wrote it to favor positive results and let it to a friendly face. Bad move, and the reason why the "Sesame Street" results were not only educationally trivial but biased toward a favorable result as well.

Fourth, that experience pointed the way to a solution, or so it appeared. The agency next lets two contracts, both of which it writes, one for program development and, independently, an evaluation contract. Here, the flaw was less obvious and considerably more of a surprise—and the lesson that we learned was very, very expensive. So who was the agency's program officer on the evaluation contract? Well, it seems to make sense to use the person who already knows all about the program. Unfortunately, no, for reasons elaborated earlier. That is someone who is already gone to bat for the program, beginning with the inescapable fact that he or she has to be its representative back at the agency ranch, going on through making the site visits and forming social ties with the program people. It is not surprising that this is someone who does not want to be the bearer of bad tidings back at the ranch where all of those favorable reports were made before. This person just will not take "no good" for an answer from the evaluation contractor and, in fact, cooks the books by requesting that the evaluation contractor make the program look better or not get signed off for the quarterly payment. So this procedure is not the solution. But we are getting closer.

Fifth, this time we set up a separate evaluation office in the agency. They get to let the evaluation contracts, supervise them, and are held accountable for professional standards in the performance of those contractors. The programs are contracted and monitored out of quite different offices. This has been a highly successful model, used in many fields, for example, in the great days of the Dallas school district under Nolan Estes, with Bill Webster running the evaluation office. Given the right players, this model is as good as it needs to be. But it is not a perfect formula. It depends on the integrity and professionalism of the players. After all, the big boss, who pays for both the evaluation office and the programs, may not want to hear—and may not want Congress (or the school board) to hear—that he or she sank a stack of money into a program that turned out badly. Surely, that investment will be interpreted as a sign of bad judgment. All too often, that fear is correct, and everyone in the agency knows it. So pressure is thereby put on the head of the evaluation office not to be the bearer of bad tidings, and we have lost our objective evaluation. We have to do better, if we can. What we have to do is lengthen the feedback loop, so that the evaluator in no significant way sees the success of the program as connected to his or her personal success.

But if we cannot do better, we must do at least this well and check that the program is being run professionally. It is not as if there is something inherently flawed about this arrangement. Nolan Estes's attitude toward Bill Webster, as far as an outsider could tell, was of the following nature: "Bill, I don't want any unpleasant surprises. I much prefer an early warning of bad news to surprises. If you are the bearer of bad news about one of our programs, I have time to work out a fix before the board gets the bad news. If bad news gets to the board directly, with no warning to me, I stand in front of them with egg on my face. I depend on you to find the bad news first—and, of course, the good news too. Don't worry about me 'killing the messenger'; you'll get your raises for thorough coverage, not for good news." We can see here that there is not even reliance on altruism or a sense of duty, just enlightened self-interest. But enlightenment is hard to find.

Finally, the sixth step is where the General Accounting Office, Office of Technology Assessment, Congressional Budget Office, the supervisory agencies such as the audit agencies, and the inspectors general come in. When those offices are run well, they are run as quality-control systems and they break the 80/20 rule for their own evaluations. And once they are in place, with a good record, the chilling effect on those thinking of getting a little sloppy with the evaluations is notable. Furthermore, they represent a role model and a source of examples of how to do evaluations well. True, they work for the federal government, just like the agencies, but the feedback loop is so long that it exerts less effect than do the positive and negative rewards from their immediate employer for doing the evaluations right.

Now, if we could just get a little more of that old trickle-down effect going! What about increased use by agencies of external evaluators rather than waiting for bad news from oversight agencies, who are, of course, external evaluators? Nice thought for us external evaluators, but therein lies a problem.

Thesis 27: External evaluators are biased toward favorable findings

It is clear that internal evaluators in the usual context are biased toward favorable findings, for the reasons already covered: either they are coauthors of the program (for example, because of formative input to it) or they work for someone whose neck is on the line with the program. But what about the external evaluator? I have mentioned the selection problem, that is, if the external evaluator is picked by the program manager, he or she is likely to be selected for friendliness. I have also mentioned the design problem, that is, if the manager can write the evaluation design, it is easy to fit in some teaching to the testing or some testing to the teaching (the design of "Sesame Street" had both). At least, there will be some social interactions—and let nature take its course ("Sesame Street" had this, too). And so on. But there are other problems that originate with the external evaluator's role.

If we start with one key economic insight about evaluation contracting, we can get a quick grip on Thesis 27. The key insight is this: No one ever got rich from one evaluation contract. It follows that repeat business is the key to success. Now, we have to have satisfied clients if we want additional business from them, and from those with whom they network. And what pleases clients more, good news about their babies or bad news? Right. So external evaluators are not a panacea, even external evaluators without direct conflicts of interest.

Looking at this whole history of bias toward favorable results, we can see that there is economic pressure toward favorable findings, social pressure and political pressure toward them, and also strong psychological pressure toward them, since being positive avoids the upsetting of others and their retaliation for those upsets. Pretty well everyone suffers from general positive bias, hence the name.

So far, then, the 80/20 rule looks like it might be optimistic. How are we ever going to get the 20 percent negative evaluations? Are they all going to come from the oversight agencies? Not at all. There will be a useful little contribution from the external contractors who get the message that certain programs are to get the hatchet.

Of course, the real world of contracted evaluations is not quite as bad as depicted here. But it is not as good as it should be, and some days it seems to be off by as large a magnitude as the difference between 8 percent true positive and 80 percent reported positive. So where can we find relief? The solution appears to be the kind of balance-of-powers approach on which the constitutional structure of this country is built. But we can put that aside for the moment and come at the problem ab initio.

Much of the positive bias comes from management's desire to get favorable reports. So it might seem that the move toward greater interaction between evaluator and evaluee, as Robert Stake and the U.K. evaluators often advocate, or toward negotiation between them (the fourth-generation viewpoint) are moves in the right direction. In such negotiations, the evaluator can keep pushing for acceptance of his or her more critical results. However, while these are moves to reduce management biases, they do little for the consumer.

One of the worst sellouts of the consumer is seen in negotiations between the management of schools, which includes the evaluators of the teachers, and the teachers' representatives. Who represents the consumers, that is, the children and the taxpayers, at these sessions? At best, someone from the school board who knows nothing about teacher evaluation. It does not help much to put students on the panel, either. This is like suggesting that the patient judge the doctor—there is an essential lack of technical skill. The school managers, who should have evaluation skills (although they usually do not), are strongly motivated by considerations of avoiding hostility, keeping the school open, deflecting criticism of themselves as incompetent managers, and so on. And they are spending some-one else's money, so they are not ideally positioned for a hard fight on behalf of those absent from the negotiating sessions. In less formal types of negotiation, the same kind of problem is often found. The negotiations are friendlier than the usual evaluator-evaluee relationship, but, unfortu-nately, what is being negotiated is someone else's birthright. Only tough independent experts running a consumer-oriented type of evaluation offer much hope of relief; and several of the biases discussed here still apply to them. In the end, we must raise the evaluation skill level all round, including that in the supervisory agencies and the press, and bring in well-trained representatives of those whose rights are at stake.

Thesis 28: Peer review panels are unreliable, fashion-biased, and manipulable

Well, now we come to the exciting part where can we trample on the most sacred of the religious icons. The unreliability claim in this thesis is not news to many people with long experience as program officers. Thanks to some of them who, led by audacious program heads, actually ran interpanel reliability tests, at least those on the grapevine know that panels are weak reeds, and we should be improving them with training and calibration. More worrisome, perhaps, is the difficulty of getting any support for this endeavor from the kingpins of the science establishment, since the effort is likely to reveal weaknesses in the system that they tout to Congress. So much for the ideals of science and truth seeking.[37]

More worrisome still, at least to us mavericks, is the problem of fashion and the bias against paradigm breakers. The evidence of this bias is overwhelming. It seems to be shared as common opinion amongst Nobelers when they get together and this matter comes up, and it is very bad news for SMET in this country. Cutting ourselves off from radically new ap-proaches that challenge the existing paradigm is sometimes right (recall the bogus claims about cold fusion), but better a hundred of those rather stimulating exercises than rejection of a couple of breakthroughs.

There are good ways to improve our proposal evaluation process to handle this bias, such as the "wild-card" system and the "special-reserve" system. In the second of these systems, after 90 percent of the money has been dispersed in the usual way, the panel votes for the best heretical proposal (or two, if they are not too expensive), using "maximum payoff if it works" as the main indicator after an entry filter on basic qualifications, with very little emphasis on the usual weight for the multiplier "probability of success." Such funding would not be provided unless plausible entries, under the special definition of plausible, are submitted; and it would not normally use up all of the remaining 10 percent of the money. There are a number of variations on this system, but something like it should be a high priority in proposal evaluation; of course, it should be treated as an experiment and two-, five-, and ten-year follow-ups should be done.

Having written all of these nice things about program officers who have done the research on peer review that evaluators should be doing, I now add that some of them have learned that comparatively modest changes in the way in which the process of proposal review is run can have large effects on the results. I know of no evidence of misuse of this information, but I deplore the lack of systematic published research on it. The best-known important craft skill here is getting panelists to write and sign their own ratings before the panel meets. This procedure greatly reduces takeovers of panel discussions by aggressive panelists, because people have more investment in their ratings; I have seen panels turned from six to one against a proposal to unanimous approval of it by people who said that they would never have bothered to fight the panels' bullies if they had not already stuck their necks out in memos that everyone had seen.

Like democracy, peer review may be a flawed system, but if given its best possible implementation, it is the best in sight and something like it will always be a key element in proposal and program evaluation. We need to correct its imperfections, and knowledge about its weaknesses is the best place to start in planning improvements.

This chapter takes a concluding look at some global considerations:
the psychology, importance, and cost of program evaluation.

Parting Perspectives

Thesis 29: The most difficult problems with program evaluation are not methodological or political but psychological

Some people do not have what it takes to be a serious evaluator or to do well with the evaluation component of a job, which involves several elements such as monitoring and development. Among those who are appointed to such positions, their shortcomings are rarely intellectual. Lack of training is common, but that is remediable; and yet even among those who have been well trained, we still find a substantial number who are completely unsatisfactory. The remaining factor is psychological, and it is usually the lack of the ability to survive outside the pack. Joining is a great human survival trait, but it is death to objectivity. As the coach says to the team in the locker room, stay mean. If people cannot play rough, they are in the wrong job. The point is not that they should always take a negative view of programs, it is that they must be able to do that and must in fact constantly rehearse that role in the early stages of evaluation, even if only to themselves. Sometimes, though, what is lacking is the ability to see the point of view of those who are at the receiving end of the evaluation—the lack of empathic skills—and that is just as important a failing.

Sooner or later, evaluators also encounter a more extreme psychological phenomenon, which they find hard to understand without forewarning. It is valuephobia, the clinical condition at the end of the spectrum of the perfectly normal phenomenon of evaluation anxiety. Some people are phobic, not just anxious, about evaluation of their programs, themselves, their children, their favorite sports teams, or their company. They will lie, cheat, or steal in order to thwart a proposal to have one of their highly valenced objects evaluated seriously, or in order to thwart the evaluation process if they cannot prevent its startup. It is startling to encounter this phobia, and one must realize immediately that this is usually not a problem that can be solved by reasoning. Evaluators must build their bridges before this condition comes up, so that they can get help in order to survive the attacks and get help as appropriate for the attackers.

The other side of this condition is that good evaluators are often in a position to be, and can helpfully be, a kind of therapist. They are, after all, like referees, outsiders who, we hope, have not formed alliances that preempt assistance to those who are drowning. One of the most persuasive analyses of psychotherapy (it was produced by a therapist) suggests that its success is solely due to its provision of a nonjudgmental listener. Competent evaluators begin their evaluations as nonjudgmental listeners, as individuals open to and able to understand both highly favorable and highly critical responses to the target programs. Of course, as listeners, they must not get seduced into doing something that they are not trained to do just because someone assumes that they can do it and wants them to do it, as when evaluators are seduced into offering recommendations though they lack the relevant expertise. But it is also important to be a human being, so one needs to consider carefully how to cope with this quasi-therapist role. Like teaching, it is an important part of the real world of being an evaluator.

The roots of resistance to evaluation go very deep indeed, and it is wise not to underestimate their strength. For many people, to concede that their work needs evaluation is to concede that they lack competence. It is part of the ego's survival repertoire to be self-sufficient. Asking someone else, even someone with demonstrable expertise, what car or computer to buy is hard for many (it is different to sneak a look at a magazine). Asking a competent other whether one's work is any good is much harder. But that is what it takes to be a professional. Not only is the failure to ask for assistance a certain sign of the amateur program manager or program developer, it is a certain sign of the amateur evaluator.

Thesis 30: Evaluation is as important as content in education programs

Once we understand that there is no chance of good education programs springing from the brow of Zeus, then we are already committed to the view that both good content and good evaluation are necessary conditions for a good program. That view is not the same as the simple claim on which everyone would agree: A good idea and some revision are always necessary. It means that we have to start early with the process of serious program evaluation, that is, evaluation using external evaluators with evaluation training, not just people with experience and subject matter expertise, although they too should be part of the evaluation process, doing more than one formative evaluation. And it means that we must systematically incorporate the evaluation feedback into materials revision. Remember what happened to the programs run by good scientists or mathematicians who were keen educators but merely went through revision cycles without looking at cost. We can hardly remember their names, although we put tens of millions of dollars into their projects. The outcome of sinking without a trace can be expected if we fail to give evaluation an equal role with superb content.

Even the easy part of an evaluation-driven development process, designing and implementing the feedback-driven iterations in the improvement cycle, is not a trivial matter. We do not have natural instincts that tell us what decisions to make about sample selection, sample size, test design and test administration controls, number of testing cycles, controls for maturation and Hawthorne effects, how to combine comments on ease of use with measures of the amount and value of the learning acquired, the use and choice of external versus internal evaluators in the formative process, and—hardest of all—what is missing from the list just given.

Genius content is not easy to find, either. Clearly, it is not the same as having genius authors because such people often cannot write for the students whom we or they are trying to reach. It is not even the same as having suitably written and highly original content, because the existing materials may be satisfactory at the grade levels in question, and any new materials are sure to displace coverage of the basics in that area. Original is no excuse for redundant; go to the needs assessment to make the distinction. Even if we construe genius content to include all cases of brilliant new ways to present material, "new and brilliant" is not the same as "produces significantly better results," let alone the same as cost-effective, let alone enough to support cost-possible. The history of the Comprehensive School Mathematics Program shows that thousands of experts—mathematicians and mathematics teachers—are willing to sign a petition supporting the addition of more taxpayer millions to an approach that is totally without value, because it was so expensive as to be completely beyond the means of schools to buy.

Simple enough distinctions, right? But the history of science, mathematics, engineering, and technology (SMET) education programs is replete with examples that violate them. Computer-assisted instruction, for example, provides a stream of object lessons in failing to make just these distinctions. There are important pockets in the K–18 curriculum where computers are superior to the best print materials, but the big push in computer-assisted instruction did not focus on those few promising targets. It went for the mainstream. The whole story of PLATO, the overenthusiasm for Writing to Read, the current efforts by Apple with computer worlds, and nearly all of the multimedia efforts are largely more of the same: extravagances driven by people without the faintest glimmering of the reality that serious evaluation makes one confront. There is a niche market for each of these products, of course, but it is a small niche and nobody bothered to define it, they were so keen to take over the universe. But a case can be made that if a program has something like genius content and highly competent evaluation, it has a minimally sufficient condition for good results, because that combination provides just enough to justify a beginning and ensure that the program will gradually improve—if it is worth improving. If it is not, then its cutoff is a good result.

This conclusion is self-reflexive. It applies to many of our own graduate training programs, not only in SMET, but in fields such as health and other social services. Do they go beyond good content related to the field to provide minimal professional training in evaluation, covering a smattering of the topics listed here? Judging from discussions with their graduates and study of catalogues from leading universities, I believe that the answer is almost always no.[38] This is hardly a good basis for the graduates to go on into careers working for programs in those fields and eventually managing them—quite often evaluating them and, more often, being accountable for the use of the funds that support them.

Thesis 31: Routine program evaluation should pay for itself

Sometimes program managers and program officers, or representatives of supervisory agencies, have to conduct or arrange evaluations for accountability reasons. Sometimes evaluations are done for research reasons. These reasons are good reasons in themselves, but they do not always lead to payoffs in the accounts of the programs that offset their costs. Instead, they require funding from outside sources. The concern here is not primarily about such evaluations but about "routine program evaluation," meaning the kind of evaluation that should be arranged by program management and program officers as part of good management of the program.[39]

Unfortunately, just because so little serious evaluation is set up and maintained as a standard function of program management, evaluation is widely thought to be represented by external ad hoc evaluations. Evaluation in that role is nearly always seen as an imposition, and, if paid for by the agency, an unfortunate diversion of resources from the direct support of services. This view is common among project staff whose project is evaluated, and it is sometimes shared by the person who does the evaluation. The view may coexist with the recognition, at an intellectual level, of the appropriateness of evaluation for reasons of quality improvement and cost reduction, causes to which program staff subscribe in principle. But the overall attitude is still at best analogous to the attitude toward checkup visits to the dentist. If program staff think of evaluation solely in terms of the external "checking up on you" role, or, at best, the "dentist" role, they are not likely to appreciate it and work hard to improve the program.

A more appropriate attitude is to realize that a serious effort at evaluation provides corrected vision for professional program management. Without it, managers are unable to see clearly something so close to them and hence unable to manage effectively. Of course, the manager sees *something* and can easily think that it is all there is to see, but that is all too likely to be just a view distorted by the myopia due to close work. Professional managers need help with evaluation—from internal and external evaluators—and know it, because professionals know their own weaknesses in judging the merit of things that they have helped to create. And professionals do not find it rewarding to create things that are then shown to be fatally flawed by summative evaluators from oversight agencies or consumer organizations.

A manager who only does evaluation at the amateur level is acting like an amateur driver in an off-road race whose view is either fixed on the far distance or on the ground just in front of the wheels. Both views are relevant to the task at hand, but neither alone will get the job done. Indeed, even back-and-forth alternation of views will not get the job done; the driver will quickly crash and burn. Learning how to give them both appropriate time slices along with the activities of continuously scanning the instrument panel, reading the maps, checking the compass, watching the sky for weather changes, monitoring the sounds of the engine and suspension for signs of trouble, calculating the average speed and comparing it to the plan (and to the minimum required to qualify for the next stage), and listening to the communications radio to pick up news of the other drivers and the whereabouts of one's own pit crew—that is the package of survival skills for the task. There is nothing surprising in the list, and nothing particularly difficult by itself, although that does not mean that they are trivial skills. Leave out any one and, sooner or later, the driver will be out of the race. And we can see immediately that it is quite a trick to keep on top of all of these tasks. Doing so is the professional driver's skill.

The professional evaluator has only two tricks. One of them is analogous to the professional driver's ability to perform a whole range of dissimilar tasks—running an evaluation checklist—and not let the performance of any subset of them get in the way of doing the others before they get out of hand. It is no mean feat, but good evaluators and good managers can do it. This is not an argument for hiring professional evaluators, it is an argument for the manager to acquire the skills of a professional evaluator. The more proficient a manager is at those skills, the less he or she will need someone else; and when outside assistance is needed, the better the manager will be at picking outside evaluators, defining their mission, determining the value of what they do, and limiting their cost.

The second trick of the professional evaluator is simply to be independent and to stay as independent as possible. This is not a trick that managers can master in their own programs, but they can get better and better at doing it, especially by practicing on other people's programs. Consequently, when they do need to cover themselves by using an external evaluator, it can often be for a day or two instead of for a month.

Evaluation evangelists should not be interested in extending their domain; they should only want to save souls. Evaluation is salvation, even if it is only a small part of salvation, for the quality of our work, for our sense of worth, for the future of our society. Evaluation involves a set of skills that managers and project officers should learn because competence requires that they be evaluators of their own projects, and of any internal evaluations run by those projects on their own work, and of any evaluations of their own work run by their own supervisors, and of any external evaluators of those projects. The internal and external evaluators of a project can do more legwork than the project manager, but he or she must be able to define, grasp, and evaluate the overview and the components of their work.

People should not get management advice or tax advice or computers for the office just to keep up with the Joneses. They should get them when doing so saves money or time in the long run or improves the quality of work or work life more than enough to cover the money costs involved. Evaluation is in the same category. People should treat it that way; expect evaluation to pay for itself, expect evaluators to show them how the evaluation (or the recommended evaluation process) will pay for itself—in savings, improvement of quality, or both. That demand will change evaluators and change evaluation, for the better.

But that is the promise of the bodybuilders when they sign us up for the weights program. Sadly, it does not mean that we shall laugh every step of the way. When this reality dawns on us is also when they say, "No pain, no gain."

NOTES

1. Some details of the many points shortchanged here are available in other ways. First, each topic is covered in Scriven, 1991, which contains a few hundred short essays in addition to lexicographical entries, source references, and an introductory essay on the nature of evaluation. (Edition 4.2+ is now available on disk and contains thirty-three thousand words more than 4.0, the hard-copy version.) Second, I can be reached for inquiries at (415) 663-1511 (Fax: 415-663-1913), or at P.O. Box 69, Point Reyes, CA 94956, or as scriven@aol.com on Internet. Comments on and criticisms of this volume are very welcome.

2. Alkin (in McLaughlin and Phillips, 1991, pp. 93–96) recently reviewed his original definition of evaluation after twenty-one years and still could not bring himself to include any reference to merit, worth, or value. He defines evaluation as the collection and presentation of data summaries for decision makers, which is, of course, the definition of management information systems.

3. This attempt to replace evaluation with explanation is reminiscent of the last stand of psychotherapists faced with the put-up or shut-up attitude of those doing outcomes studies in the 1950s and 1960s. They tried to replace remediation with explanation, arguing that the payoff from psychotherapy was improved understanding by the patients of their conditions, rather than symptoms reduction. This was not a popular view among patients who were in pain and paying to reduce it.

4. That is, at issue are statements such as "If you value so-and-so, then this will be a good program for you," "The program was very successful in meeting its goals," or "If technology education should be as easily accessible to girls as it is to boys, then this program will help bring that about." These claims, which are simple examples, of course, express evaluative conclusions only relative to the clients' or the consumers' values. A direct evaluative claim, by contrast, states, "This program is not cost-effective compared to the use of traditional methods," "This is the best of the options," or "These side effects are extremely unfortunate." Note that the first of these latter examples is comparative, which is completely different from relativistic.

5. The reference here is to the infamous Astin case, where the director of the National Bureau of Standards was asked to do a study of the effect of the battery additive AD-X2 prior to government's purchase of it for the agency's vehicle fleet. The additive had no effect, as was apparent from a simple control-group study of government vehicles, and Astin's report of that result cost him his job (although media pressure eventually got him reinstated). A look at the process of evaluation for textbooks and its

political ambience provides what may be an even clearer example of product evaluation involving the same problems as found in program evaluation.

6. Definitions of functional entities such as scientific explanations and experimental designs, like those of washing machines, personal computers, and computer literacy programs, usually include references to the entities' functions and thus *definitionally* provide the dimensions along which their merit can be assessed. Hence, the factual data on relative performance can often entail a rating or ranking, that is, evaluative conclusions. The process does not always provide a ranking, and to establish one, it is sometimes necessary to turn to a needs assessment that establishes the relative importance of the dimensions of merit in a particular case. The needs assessment can be done with a high degree of objectivity (for example, by using fault tree charts, testing, and analysis of job entry requirements). Sometimes, too, we add "universal" criteria of merit, for example, minimizing of environmental damage, to the definitional criteria. We can readily give good reasons for doing that. The whole process is commonsensical enough, whether applied to travel alarms or chemistry curricula.

7. There were other logical errors in the values-free doctrine, notably the following three: (1) There was the error of thinking that the impossibility of deducing value conclusions from factual premises—and what was thought to be the even more obvious impossibility of inducing them— meant that there was no way of legitimately inferring them. (They can be inferred using probative logic, the logic of prime facie inference and the paradigm of legal reasoning.) (2) There was the view that one can establish factual premises without any use of evaluative premises. (One needs to establish the validity of the observations and inference rules, an evaluative process.) And (3) there was the hierarchical view of epistemology, that is, the view that there are ultimate premises on which all knowledge claims rest. Knowledge is a network or web structure, and the fact that the establishment of factual conclusions requires evaluative premises does not mean that the ultimate premises are evaluative; evaluative premises can be established through factual data in an iterative, noncircular process, which we can and often do replay upon challenge, as well as through definitions. Connected with the first of these errors was the mistake of thinking that the connections between the terms in a definition and the term defined must be those of logical necessity. Only a criterial connection is necessary, and this is in fact the normal link between terms used in common—and scientific—parlance and the terms used to define them, for example, between temperature and the sensation of heat, intelligence and problem solving ability, apples and apple trees. Criterial connections support prima facie inferences and hence are another part of the territory explored by probative logic (see Scriven, 1991).

8. There was a tiny minority that challenged this retreat to the ivory tower:

Russell Lynd, C. Wright Mills, and Kurt Lewin are perhaps the most important examples. Mills's position was interesting in that he wanted social scientists to stay away from involvement with government programs; but this was not because he wanted them to avoid studying the programs, only that he wanted them to retain their objectivity.

9. A notable exception to this trend is the history of the Personalized System of Instruction approach (the Keller Plan). Its supporters were considerably more serious about evaluation than were most other efforts in science education, and the results were enlightening, although not unqualifiedly supportive. Preliminary figures suggest that of all the federally funded projects in the education area of science, math, engineering, and technology, located in twelve federal agencies, only about 10 percent can even identify the size of the group they have affected directly, and only about 12 percent of the projects have an evaluation that the parent agency is prepared to put forward. The quality of the evaluations for the 12 percent of course vary, but these figures show that one in six of them does not include a reliable estimate of the size of the affected group, usually one of the most accessible facts that an evaluator must obtain.

10. As the terms are commonly used, *projects* refers here to the molecules that constitute programs. They are individual implementations on particular sites. Project components, such as materials development, training, and management, are the atoms that make up the project molecules. *Agency* refers to a macromolecule, a combination of programs.

11. With respect to evaluator independence, reviewers for the enthusiast magazines are suspect to the extent that they are influenced by the magazines' dependence on advertising by the manufacturers of the products that they are reviewing. But several publications, for example, *Consumer Reports,* accept no advertising.

12. It is an advantage of goal-free methodology that it is reversible, so that if an evaluation is started in that mode, or with one or two staff operating in that mode, one can proceed to the point of a preliminary report (from those individuals) and nevertheless include a goal-based final phase (or parallel phase). Goal-based evaluations, on the other hand, are not reversible. One cannot decide to forget the goals of the program and start over in goal-free mode.

13. Of course, in product evaluation, say, of a car, we can tell that the goals of the designers included construction of a car, or even, sometimes, construction of a luxury four-seater passenger car. We can tell this, but we should not use it for evaluation. What if they really wanted it to be a five-seater, although it is obvious to us that the car cannot comfortably seat five people? This intent simply does not matter in the evaluation of the car from our point of view. Furthermore, we cannot tell and do not care about what they were trying to do that was different from the competition. It is those goals, not the most generic goal ("making a car"), that we ignore in a goal-

free mode, that is, a normal product evaluation mode. We only care about how the car suits us (fits our needs and preferences). The same is true of a mathematics program for a ninth-grade class. Anyone can see that it is a mathematics program; it is the rest that we do not need to know about—and do better not to know about.

14. In this area of evaluation, SMET people feel entirely comfortable because they are used to reviewing texts for courses that they teach in their subject matter specialties. Unfortunately, it has never occurred to them that they were doing evaluation and that it was simply their lack of relevant expertise, not the logic of the matter, that precluded this activity throughout the entire domain of program evaluation.

15. Of course, the critical competitor may not be medieval. A good example is the continued (apparent) invincibility of the best of the programmed texts for teaching reading. Despite wave after wave of later fashions, the only real horse races that have been run, to the best of my knowledge, show the programmed text to be far the best approach for a broad spectrum of students. As an enthusiastic techno-junkie and veteran of many substantial evaluations of educational technology, such as PLATO, videodisks, computer literacy programs, and video games, I think that there are a number of niches where technology can produce enormous advances over traditional approaches. But in many of the best-known cases, for example, "Sesame Street" and Writing to Read, the widely publicized favorable evaluations have been invalid and the proper conclusion goes against the innovation (in these cases, television and computer-assisted instruction).

16. They can still do a great deal of work involved in program evaluation, and there will be some cases where what they do is an evaluation de facto, given the context. But at the end of the day, most days, the client needs to know whether the program does work well, just as he or she needs to know if the bridge will hold the projected traffic—not that it would *if* ten conditions hold. It is the evaluator's responsibility, just as it is the civil engineer's, to find out if those conditions currently hold or will hold. Of course, it is always possible that an evaluator, like an engineer, will be wrong in that determination, but that is not the issue here. The question is whether one can be right often enough to justify betting the costs of the project and the welfare of the users. If the evaluator cannot pass that test, the evaluation will be of no more use than a hypothetical bridge design that no engineer will endorse for a given site.

17. In the area of SMET education programs, two types of personnel evaluation are particularly important: teacher evaluation and student evaluation. It is common to suppose that the evaluation of student knowledge, attitudes, and skills, which is certainly a subdiscipline in educational psychology and hence social science, is the same as the evaluation of students. However, only the latter is personnel evaluation, and it involves

significantly more than the former, for example, it involves assessing aspects of character as well as the difficult process of synthesizing all of the component data.

18. We have seen the pendulum swing wildly on this point. Cook (in McLaughlin and Phillips, 1991) provides the most balanced recent overview. While there are certainly areas where true control groups are impossible in evaluation studies, as in other research, most of the arguments that they are rarely feasible for evaluation designs have been disproved by experience, and, where feasible, such studies are clearly well ahead of even the next best quasi-experimental designs. There is nothing special about evaluation investigations with respect to the issue of true experimental designs, so no thesis about that subject is included in my set.

19. In a recent monograph, Paul Spector defines summated rating scales, widely used in Likert's version for affective measurement, as having four characteristics, one of which is that there is no "right" answer to an item. Unpacking this condition, he says, "Summated rating scales cannot be used to test for knowledge or ability." But his own Work Locus of Control Scale, like most Likert-type scales, violates this condition in two ways. Since each response represents a claim about what the respondent believes (for example, "Agree very strongly"), it is an autobiographical claim and can clearly be right or wrong, the latter either because the respondent is lying or because he or she is low on self-knowledge. Perhaps this apparent violation is not relevant because of the quotes that Spector puts around "right." Second, many of the items in fact have correct and incorrect answers, sometimes even in the set of allowed responses. For example, one of his items is, "If you know what you want out of a job, you can find a job that gives it to you." There are several hundred thousand unemployed in this country who can prove that this statement is false. Someone who responds "Agree very much" is showing ignorance, hence lack of knowledge, contrary to his condition. This kind of conceptual sloppiness does not survive serious evaluative investigation.

20. It is also true that subject matter specialists often miss the presuppositions of current approaches to their discipline, as the deconstructionists point out. Someone with expertise in critical thinking ("informal logic" is the name of the discipline that has emerged) is the best bet on this point.

21. The methodology of the Chinese civil service examinations was quite sophisticated. Not only were examination papers coded by numbers to avoid bias from name recognition, but each was copied by a scribe to avoid calligraphic recognition as well.

22. The recently issued fifth edition of *Measurement and Evaluation in Psychology and Education* (Thorndike, 1990), which is probably the most widely used text in educational measurement, has no reference at all to the evaluation of anything or anyone in education or psychology except students.

23. There are certainly expert *specialist* product evaluators in subfields such as computer product evaluation. There are (apparently) no expert specialist proposal evaluators, only experts in subject matter fields who have extensive experience in product evaluation, which is a very different matter (they have not developed valid systematic approaches).

24. We owe this finding to some dedicated truth seekers among the National Science Foundation staff who set up parallel reviews, not to the professions, who really did not want to hear that they were (fairly) incompetent. This situation perfectly parallels that in personnel evaluation, especially in personnel selection, where almost everyone likes sitting on selection committees (if there are not too many of them) and almost no one in the SMET research areas has even the most elementary knowledge of the crucial findings of researchers who have looked at what works and fails in the process of rating and, especially, interviewing. The research makes clear that the usual interviews are guaranteed to be extremely poor selection devices (see Eder and Ferris, 1989).

25. Many years ago, in a bird park on the island of Hawai'i, I saw a young woman wearing a T-shirt with the message "A woman without a man is like a fish without a bicycle." I have been trying to think of an appropriate response ever since and have nearly decided that there is not one. On the principle that "if you can't lick 'em, join 'em," I turned the message to its present use.

26. The Colorado School of Mines once made a serious and expensive effort to get responses from their graduates to help with an evaluation of teaching and curriculum. They achieved less than a 20 percent return rate. Of course, no serious decisions can be based on that low of a return rate, since the respondents may well be atypical, a possibility that cannot be thoroughly eliminated by studies of the demographics of the nonresponders when they are such a large proportion of the target group.

27. Of course, selection by merit does not mean slavish ranking by scores on some standardized instrument such as the Scholastic Aptitude Test, since errors of measurement and invalidity mean that merit does not map directly onto those scores. Usually, it is necessary to (1) supplement the test scores with other measures of relevant aspects of merit and worth not covered by the test, (2) rank on the combined score using a validated combinatorial algorithm or heuristics, (3) identify the bridging group of candidates, that is, those with scores within the error of measurement range of the prima facie cutting score, and (4) iterate the process to select the best from this group.

28. Note that Cronbach and others' (1980) Thesis 51 sounds a little like support for this position and a recantation of their earlier attacks on summative evaluation: "An evaluation of a particular project has its greatest importance for projects that will be put in place in the future." And in their Thesis 56 we find, "The evaluator is essentially a historian."

Historical evaluation is surely only summative, since one can hardly hope to improve what is now finished.

29. In response to my first published criticisms of his claims about the relative unimportance of comparative and summative evaluation, Cronbach once asked me whether I had ever actually done an evaluation. Well, of course, philosophers (which I had been for much of my career up to that time) pride themselves on not having to actually do things in order to talk about them, but in fact I had done a number of program evaluations, and program meta-evaluations, at that point. Clearly, it had never occurred to Cronbach that every thinking adult has done many serious evaluations (of major purchases, life choices, graduate school programs, and so on), that every professor has done many more (of students, research work, texts, curricula, candidates), and that those evaluations might have exactly the same logic as the limited kind of program evaluation that he had in mind. What evaluation needed at that point (c. 1972), and for the next twenty years, was not theoreticians with more practical experience but rather theoreticians with better theories. Einstein did very little travel at the velocity of light and never made any effort to determine its exact value, but he still managed to be quite illuminating about it.

30. It is therefore discouraging to hear members of teachers' organizations demand that their contracts contain the guarantee that evaluation will only be formative. Since valid formative evaluation requires *at least* early-warning summative, summative is a no-cost option, and to reject it is the clearest possible demonstration that the teachers wish to avoid accountability and hence renounce any claim to the status of professionals. Albert Shanker, president of the American Federation of Teachers, understands the essential connections here very well and has shown considerable leadership in arguing for responsible and valid summative teacher evaluation.

31. Although the apportionment problem is seen by many as the problem to which the science of economics is a solution ("the allocation of scarce resources between competing demands"), it is difficult to find any treatment of it as a practical problem in economics textbooks.

32. The exception is if there is no time to get direct measures of performance for the individual, which happens in very rare cases. This circumstance justifies the use of empirically validated nonsimulation tests in selecting from very large numbers of applicants for a few jobs, such as when the U.S. Army had to deal with thousands of volunteers and draftees every day in gearing up for World War II.

33. In fact, the new wave in teacher evaluation involved the introduction of many "style" indicators to the observation process that came from research on teaching effectiveness, for example, high eye contact, high question asking, and high time-on-task. Not only are these so-called indicators illicit, but the use of any of them contaminates the evaluation

instrument, invalidating it although it may involve many legitimate indicators.

34. Until 1976, there was apparently no attempt anywhere to look into this crucial algorithm. At that point, a few social scientists began work on multiple-attribute utility analysis, which is potentially relevant to evaluation; however, they were hampered by their own restrictions, limiting themselves to relativistic evaluation (that is, only using the values of others and never drawing evaluative conclusions) and not looking at practical product evaluation for examples and, especially, counterexamples (see Carroll and Johnson, 1990). Other weaknesses were inappropriate assumptions about the measurement scales, a willingness to accept illicit values, and a naive view about the ability of decision makers to identify relevant criteria and determine appropriate weights.

35. What is the proof of this rule? It is a combination of direct and indirect evidence. The direct evidence is simply judgmental, based on examination of perhaps one thousand program evaluation designs and reports. Indirect evidence comes from the analogy of the quite well supported conclusion that published research (that is, research published anywhere) follows the "80/20 or worse" rule (at least 80 percent of it was not worth publishing). The argument is that it is at least as hard to create and run a worthwhile new program as to do worthwhile research. Those with experience in the research and development process are probably more likely than are researchers to agree with this rule. The second line of argument is set out in Chapter Six.

36. Nevertheless, this model is closely analogous to the practice of having teachers set and mark the tests for their own students, and it is why Oxford and Swarthmore do not allow it in their advanced programs, and why parents are right to get nervous about attempts to ditch state assessment.

37. For the science establishment not to initiate scientific studies of the validity of the means whereby they dispense billions of dollars of public money is irresponsible and self-interested, a simple abandonment of fundamental scientific practice and ethics. To argue against such studies on the grounds that they might turn up bad results out of which politicians could make "cheap political capital" and hence reduce the money going to science, which would of course be bad for the country, is a rationalization that belongs in the same category as J. Edgar Hoover's defense of his practice of blackmailing politicians in order to keep the agency's budget expanding—roughly, "It's in the interest of the country, and that's more important than the comfort of one or two miscreants."

38. After advertising widely to fill a position on my staff recently, requesting a "researcher/program evaluator, with Ph.D.," I found that many of the substantial number of applicants with doctorates from outstanding universities had done and were continuing several years of work in evaluation for state and federal agencies. However, they had no idea of the existence of

the American Evaluation Association or local organizations of professional evaluators; they had no knowledge of the standard journals and anthologies in the field (which contain many reports and methodological discussions from their own fields); and their notion of debates about models of evaluation was limited to the quantitative versus qualitative argument.

39. "Arranged by" includes the practice of having staff do the evaluation on a systematic and professional basis, including supervised field trials, but the reference is also to the commissioning of some kind of external evaluation because a professional can hardly suppose that authors are the best reviewers of books. Hence, it would be misleading to call routine program evaluation an internal evaluation; it is internally initiated, partly internally done, and partly externally done. Of course, it is formative rather than summative evaluation, which is a different issue.

REFERENCES

Carroll, J. S., and Johnson, E. J. *Decision Research: A Field Guide to Studying Decision Behavior.* Newbury Park, Calif.: Sage, 1990.

Chen, H.-T. *Theory-Driven Evaluations.* Newbury Park, Calif.: Sage, 1990.

Cronbach, L. J., Ambron, S. R., Dornbusch, S. M., Hess, R. D., Hornik, R. C., Phillips, D. C., Walker, D. F., Weiner, S. S. *Toward Reform of Program Evaluation: Aims, Methods, and Institutional Arrangements.* San Francisco: Jossey-Bass, 1980.

Eder, R. W., and Ferris, G. R. (eds.). *The Employment Interview: Theory, Research, and Practice.* Newbury Park, Calif.: Sage, 1989.

Guba, E. G. (ed.). *The Paradigm Dialog.* Newbury Park, Calif.: Sage, 1990.

Guba, E. G., and Lincoln, Y. S. *Fourth Generation Evaluation.* Newbury Park, Calif.: Sage, 1989.

House, E. R. *Evaluating with Validity.* Newbury Park, Calif.: Sage, 1980.

Joint Committee on Standards for Educational Evaluation. *Standards for Evaluations of Educational Programs.* New York: McGraw-Hill, 1980.

Joint Committee on Standards for Educational Evaluation Staff. *The Personnel Evaluation Standards: How to Assess Systems for Evaluating Educators.* Newbury Park, Calif.: Sage, 1988.

Levin, H. M. *Cost-Effectiveness: A Primer.* Newbury Park, Calif.: Sage, 1983.

McLaughlin, M. W., and Phillips, D. C. (eds.). *Evaluation and Education: At Quarter Century.* Ninetieth Yearbook of the National Society for the Study of Education Series: Part 2. Chicago: University of Chicago Press, 1991.

Morrison, D. E., and Henkel, R. E. *The Significance Test Controversy: A Reader.* Hawthorne, N.Y.: Aldine de Gruyter, 1970.

Rosenzweig, M. R., and Porter, L. W. (eds.). *Annual Review of Psychology.* Vol.42. Palo Alto, Calif.: Annual Reviews, 1991.

Rossi, P. H., and Freeman, H. E. *Evaluation: A Systematic Approach.* (4th ed.) Newbury Park, Calif.: Sage, 1989.

Scriven, M. *Primary Philosophy.* New York: McGraw-Hill, 1966.

Scriven, M. "Fallacies of Statistical Substitution." In J. Woods (ed.), *Argumentation.* Dordrecht, Netherlands: Reidel, 1988.

Scriven, M. *Evaluation Thesaurus.* (4th ed.) Newbury Park, Calif.: Sage, 1991.

Stufflebeam, D. L. (ed.). *Educational Evaluation and Decision Making.* Itasca, Ill.: Peacock, 1971.

Thorndike, R. *Projects and Materials Measurement and Evaluation in Psychology and Education.* (5th ed.) New York: Macmillan, 1990.

INDEX

ORDERING INFORMATION

NEW DIRECTIONS FOR PROGRAM EVALUATION is a series of paperback books that presents the latest techniques and procedures for conducting useful evaluation studies of all types of programs. Books in the series are published quarterly in Spring, Summer, Fall, and Winter and are available for purchase by subscription and individually.

SUBSCRIPTIONS for 1993 cost $48.00 for individuals (a savings of 34 percent over single-copy prices) and $70.00 for institutions, agencies, and libraries. Please do not send institutional checks for personal subscriptions. Standing orders are accepted.

SINGLE COPIES cost $17.95 when payment accompanies order. (California, New Jersey, New York, and Washington, D.C., residents please include appropriate sales tax.) Billed orders will be charged postage and handling.

DISCOUNTS for quantity orders are available. Please write to the address below for information.

ALL ORDERS must include either the name of an individual or an official purchase order number. Please submit your order as follows:
    Subscriptions: specify series and year subscription is to begin
    Single copies: include individual title code (such as PE1)

MAIL ALL ORDERS TO:
    Jossey-Bass Publishers
    350 Sansome Street
    San Francisco, California 94104

FOR SINGLE-COPY SALES OUTSIDE OF THE UNITED STATES CONTACT:
    Maxwell Macmillan International Publishing Group
    866 Third Avenue
    New York, New York 10022

FOR SUBSCRIPTION SALES OUTSIDE OF THE UNITED STATES, contact any international subscription agency or Jossey-Bass directly.

OTHER TITLES AVAILABLE IN THE
NEW DIRECTIONS FOR PROGRAM EVALUATION SERIES
William R. Shadish, *Editor-in-Chief*